*Unlocking the Secrets of Time*

# Unlocking the Secrets of Time

## *Maryland's Hidden Heritage*

JEAN B. RUSSO, EDITOR

THE MARYLAND HISTORICAL SOCIETY

© 1991 Jean B. Russo

This volume is published by the Maryland Historical Society, with assistance from the Maryland Humanities Council and the Maryland State Archives.

# Contents

Preface   vii

Introduction   1
NAOMI COLLINS

Reflections on the Art of History   4
GREGORY A. STIVERSON

The Carrolls   13

Clues to the Past   30

Interpreting the Past   74

The Future of the Past: An Evaluation   89
GEORGE H. CALLCOTT

Exploring the Past   94
JEAN B. RUSSO

Conference Participants   105

Index   107

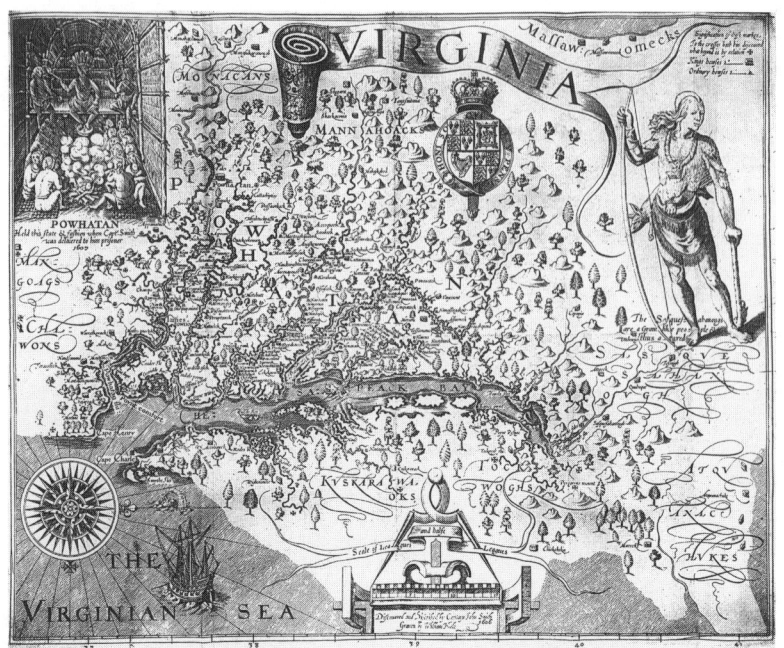

We learn about the culture of Native Americans from artifacts recovered through archaeological excavations, from descriptions in diaries and travel accounts, and from drawings such as those of a Susquehannock warrior and a Powhatan council used by Capt. John Smith as illustrations for his 1608 map of the Chesapeake Bay region.

# *Preface*

This volume is an outgrowth of a conference, "Unlocking the Secrets of Time: Maryland's Hidden Heritage," held in Annapolis, Maryland, in November 1989, under the sponsorship of the Maryland Humanities Council. Funding for the conference came from the National Endowment for the Humanities and from the Maryland State Archives as its Fourth Conference on Maryland. Support from the Maryland Department of Housing and Community Development also helped to make this conference possible.

The gathering brought together historians, archaeologists, and curators to consider several related questions: how we know what we know about the past, what we should preserve of the present to enable future generations to learn about us, and how discoveries in the future may change our views of the past. A complete list of all participants and their subjects is included as an appendix to this volume.

In order to share more broadly and in a more lasting format the insightful presentations offered in Annapolis, the papers have been gathered for publication in this volume. Rather than reprinting each paper in its entirety, the texts have been edited to provide several case studies of the ways in which scholars use evidence. The first study focuses on one historian's quest to uncover the origins of the Maryland state flag and the meaning of its elements. The second examines the ways by which different scholars, with varying interpretive needs, have explored the history of one of Maryland's most prominent families. The third study focuses on different types of evidence and the insights that they provide, particularly for exploring the histories of groups of ordinary people who do not leave the elegant houses or extensive papers that make members of the elite much easier topics of study. The final case study considers the sources and uses of evidence that is shared with the public in a museum setting, whether it be through living history programs, exhibits, or catalogs. Two concluding sections first evaluate the current status of the pursuit of history in the context of the papers presented at the conference and then offer suggestions to the reader, both for further exploration of the theme and for ways to begin as individuals to "unlock the secrets of time."

*Unlocking the Secrets of Time*

*This 1870 lithograph marks passage of the Fifteenth Amendment to the Constitution, which guaranteed the right to vote to all male citizens. The central portion of the lithograph depicts the parade held by Baltimore blacks to celebrate the event, while the border vignettes illustrate persons and institutions instrumental in securing freedom and civil rights for the nation's blacks. Artifacts such as this lithograph give voice to the historical experience of groups whose lives are less likely to be preserved in more traditional records.*

# Introduction

## NAOMI COLLINS

In November 1989, the Maryland Humanities Council developed and produced a conference, "Unlocking the Secrets of Time: Maryland's Hidden Heritage," in response to the great interest Marylanders have shown in knowing their own history. "Unlocking the Secrets" took participants to the root of history by exploring how the story of our past is formed. It examined the ways in which letters, diaries, and newspapers; prints, drawings, and photographs; portraits, artifacts, and implements reveal the lives of those who lived before us. Although the program could not explore these questions definitively, we hoped that it would stimulate an interest in new ways of thinking about the past and the future, addressing broad questions about how we can know more about ourselves.

The program was inspired, in part, by my good fortune in spending some years, beginning in graduate school, exploring the period of England's civil wars of the seventeenth century. The surviving sources for that time and place, the remnants those English men and women left behind, are like the pieces of a jigsaw puzzle: three-hundred-year-old notes, diaries, letters bound in red ribbons, fiery sermons, roughly printed broadsides driven by the force and immediacy (and the intemperateness) of inspired revolutionaries. Supplementing these random findings, the staid records in the archives and public record offices—official rolls and cases, accounts and documents of parliaments and princes, courts and legislatures, and boards and commissions—provided other clues. Paintings, prints, etchings, and drawings opened yet other windows onto the past, with glimpses into homes and farms, feasts and battles, offering insights into the lives of people and places, as well as into the mind and vision of the artists who portrayed them.

Following the delight in discovery came the challenge of interpreting the materials. All the finds were surrounded in mystery, limited by chance, discovered through serendipity; they hinted at meanings, teased with missing pieces and tantalizing gaps. What did these remnants mean? Were they typical? Significant? Did they survive because they were important—or because they were unimportant? (Those pristine, leather-bound volumes of classics lining the shelves of the grand libraries of the well-to-do homes: were they clues to what people read or were they decorative, rarely if ever read, and therefore spared the deterioration that would accompany frequent use?)

After figuring out the significance of each clue, the next step was to piece the parts together to create a coherent, convincing picture of the past. Fitting together the concrete pieces with the surmises that bridged the gaps, a story emerged to explain what happened three hundred years ago. But as satisfying as this resolution was, it was clear that the story of those complex times was built on the evidence at hand as I wrote. With time, the discovery of new materials might confirm or change this vision; through time, our understanding of the past evolves.

As I worked, I could also imagine how each day we ourselves determine what future historians will have to work with, how what we leave behind today—and what we don't—will be the clues and the gaps from which searchers in the twenty-first century will have to create a picture of our own day. One wonders how people will deal with so much material—and so little. Massive amounts of print material and other records will crowd their desks, vying for attention, while first drafts of poems, books, and treaties will be scarce, the final versions having been wordprocessed to perfection, eliminating traces of earlier thoughts.

If you have wondered about the ways we seek, find, and interpret the remnants of the past to create a picture of other times—how we know about the towns and the people that preceded us; how we learn about the lives not only of national leaders, but of factory workers and farmers; of men, women, and children; of people of different backgrounds and origins—we invite you to explore these questions with the scholars who participated in our program. Through the essays in this volume, you can delve one step deeper than in traditional historical works to explore how the past reveals itself to us in the present, and how the mystery of the past is solved through the clues that survive today.

# Reflections on the Art of History
## GREGORY A. STIVERSON

One way to understand the pursuit and use of historical evidence is through a look at how an individual can use a variety of clues to solve a historical puzzle. Assistant State Archivist Gregory Stiverson faced such a puzzle when asked to answer a seemingly straightforward question: what was the origin of the banner now legally defined as the Maryland flag? Answering the question, it developed, required both intuition and detective work.

The Maryland flag consists of four quarters drawn directly from the shield in the coat-of-arms of the Calverts, the proprietary family that was granted the charter to Maryland in 1632. The yellow and black with the diagonal band of alternating colors are the Calvert colors. The red and white with the bottony cross design come from the coat-of-arms of George Calvert's maternal family, the Crosslands. So, the Maryland flag is simply the alternating Calvert and Crossland colors as represented in the shield of the Calvert family coat-of-arms.

Knowing the source of the Maryland flag's design does not, however, answer the question of when the Maryland flag in its present form came about. Throughout the colonial period, only the yellow and black colors of the Calvert family were used on flags. This made sense, because it was the Calvert family, not the Crosslands, who were proprietors of Maryland. In fact, it was not until after the Civil War that a banner in the form of the present Maryland flag can be documented. So the task was to determine why, more than two and a half centuries after the Calverts had founded Maryland and a century after the proprietorship had ended with the Declaration of Independence, Marylanders turned to a banner incorporating the Calvert and Crossland colors as a symbol for the state.

What I was able to determine from a variety of sources was that when the Southern states seceded, Marylanders who remained loyal to the Union identified themselves and celebrated Maryland's remaining in the Union by flying the ancient yellow and black colors, which they called the "Maryland colors" or "Baltimore colors." This left those Marylanders who supported the South, and especially those citizens of the state who went south to fight for the Confederacy, without an identifying mark or banner for their state.

These Southern sympathizers turned to the Crossland quadrants in the old proprietary coat-of-arms both for identifying colors—red and white—and, for a readily identifiable symbol, the cross bottony. After the war, the red and white colors and the cross bottony appeared with increasing frequency in Maryland, especially after the new state constitution, adopted in 1867, enabled the Democrats, many of whom were former Confederates

*Reflections on the Art of History*

(Right) *This drawing by Maryland artist Franklin B. Mayer provides the earliest visual documentation for the present form of the Maryland flag.*

(Below left) *This photo of Marylander Bradley Johnson, a Confederate general, shows him with a cross bottony pin as part of his uniform.*

(Below right) *Memorial pins and ribbons worn by Confederate veterans from Maryland featured the cross bottony and red and white colors.*

Unlocking the Secrets of Time

or Confederate sympathizers, to take control of the government.

By 1889, the state's leading militia unit, the Fifth Maryland Regiment, which had been formed in 1867 by former Confederates, adopted a flag joining the yellow and black Calvert colors with the red and white Crossland colors in the cross bottony design. By 1904, this banner was so well known that the General Assembly adopted it as the state flag, a symbol not only of the state's long history dating back to the original proprietorship of the Calverts, but also as a symbol of the reunion of all the state's citizens in the aftermath of the divisive Civil War.

That was my conclusion about the origin of our state flag, but there was really no documentary evidence to support it. Instead, I turned to other kinds of evidence in my research, demonstrating just how many different kinds of things can help us better understand our state's history.

A photograph of the Fifth Maryland Regiment, serving as an escort to the governor of Maryland at the dedication of the Maryland monument on the Gettysburg battlefield in October 1888, has long been thought to be the earliest documentation of the Maryland flag in its present form, and has also been used as proof that the flag had a military origin, that is, with the Fifth Regiment. One day I accidentally happened upon a Frank B. Mayer drawing, however, which shows part of the huge parade held in Baltimore in October 1880 to celebrate the 150th anniversary of that city. Mayer depicted the Maryland flag in its present form (although displayed incorrectly according to present law), verifying that the design was known at least eight years before the Gettysburg ceremony and that it was used in a civilian parade unrelated to the Fifth Regiment.

Once I had established that the Maryland flag dated from at least 1880, I had to prove the connection between the red and white Crossland colors and the cross bottony and Confederate sympathies during the Civil War. We know that at least a few Confederate soldiers from Maryland wore lapel pins in the cross bottony shape to identify their state of origin. Two of these pins are in the Confederate Museum in Richmond and several others are owned by private collectors. A postwar photograph of Maryland's most famous Confederate general, Bradley Johnson of Frederick, shows a cross bottony pin over his heart. General Johnson, in fact, may have been the most influential in popularizing the red and white colors and cross bottony design as an emblem for Marylanders serving in the Confederate army. His headquarters flag, now also in the Confederate Museum's collection, shows the use of both the cross bottony design and the red and white colors.

After the war, Confederates returning home to Maryland perpetuated the use of the red and white colors and the cross bottony. The entrance gate to the Maryland Line Confederate Soldier's Home, which opened in June 1888 in Pikesville, featured a huge cross bottony. A Baltimore native, Charles Kettlewell, who served in the Confederate cavalry and who was very active in veterans' organizations after the war, saved his Confederate veterans' memorabilia. His collection includes many ribbons produced for Confederate States of America veterans' events, featuring the red and white colors, the cross bottony, or both. One pin joins a red and white ribbon and the top portion of the cross bottony to the Confederate "stars and bars." A memorial ribbon for a former Confederate officer, James R. Herbert, who became the first colonel of the Fifth Regiment when it was formed in 1867, depicts his tombstone with a cross bottony on the top. Another ribbon combines the red and white colors with a pin showing Gen. Robert E. Lee, while a third joins the red and white colors and the cross bottony. A final example, a pin and ribbon produced by Sisco Brothers Flag Company of Baltimore for the Robert E. Lee monument dedication ceremony in 1890, brings together all the elements of the state flag: the Calvert and Crossland colors and the Crossland cross.

I fashioned my argument about the origins of the Maryland state flag from these kinds of evidence—not the best kinds, at least for someone who is more comfortable with documentary sources, but still quite compelling when all the pieces are pulled together. And at this point in my research, another kind of evidence was brought to my attention that helped reinforce the argument.

When the Southern states began to secede in the spring of 1861, the Baltimore newspapers reported numerous instances of Confederate sympathizers raising "Southern colors" and wearing ribbons and other articles of attire in red and white to show their sympathy with the South. The federal government could not permit Maryland to secede, and troops were sent to Baltimore to quell dissent. The newspapers contain many references to federal troops under the command of Gen. John Dix closing down stores that displayed socks, cravats, and other items colored red and white, but some of the stories seem so ludicrous that it is

*This red and white dress and the note accompanying it provided the final link associating the Crossland colors of red and white with support for the Confederate cause.*

difficult to put much faith in them. A popular song of the day, for example, entitled "Dix's Manifesto," included the verse:

> On Barber's pole, and mint stick;
> He did his veto place;
> He swore that in his city;
> He'd red and white erase.

10    Unlocking the Secrets of Time

Could the federal authorities have been so offended by the red and white Crossland colors that they would consider barbers and candy vendors traitors?

As I noted, I received some new evidence that tends to confirm the federal authorities' determination to rid Baltimore of all traces of red and white. The Maryland Historical Society sent me slides of one of their recent acquisitions, a lovely little red and white silk taffeta dress, which had been authenticated to the period of the Civil War. What is most fascinating, however, is the contemporary note pinned to the back of the dress, which tells the story of why this new and quite beautiful garment was stored away and preserved by the family. The note reads:

> During the Civil War, the federal soldiers were stationed in Baltimore and Clara Teleiback, then 4 years old, started to Sunday school with this dress on *new*.

The note continues on the back:

> and the soldiers made her come back and take it off as it was red white and red, the southern colors, calling her a rebel.

Surely for this little four-year-old girl and her family, the red and white colors would always remind them of the oppression they had endured, the same as the red and white colors and cross bottony reminded Maryland-born former Confederates of their sacrifices in a losing cause. Those experiences during the Civil War gave the Crossland colors and bottony cross a special meaning to many Marylanders, and the emergence of a new state banner that added the Crossland colors and cross bottony design to the traditional yellow and black must

*Reflections on the Art of History*

have been a welcome symbol of progress in the slow process of healing wounds and pulling Maryland society back together.

These images help underline my central point: history can be reconstructed from many different kinds of evidence and each has validity in providing a better and fuller explanation of our past.

# The Carrolls

The Carrolls were one of the preeminent families during Maryland's colonial and early national periods, occupying a position of economic dominance, social prestige, and political influence equalled by few others. Both the Protestant and Catholic Carrolls (distant cousins) left a tangible legacy to later generations, in the form of artifacts and documents. The two homes of the Protestant Carrolls, that of Dr. Charles Carroll in Annapolis and of his son, Charles Carroll, Barrister at Mt. Clare in Baltimore, survive, as does a large collection of family papers. Doughoregan Manor in Howard County, the family seat of the Catholic Carrolls, the branch with which this chapter concerns itself, remains privately held in the Carroll family. Carroll House in Annapolis, built by Charles Carroll of Annapolis; Carroll Mansion in Baltimore, the last town home of his son, Charles Carroll of Carrollton; and Homewood House, the home financed by Charles Carroll of Carrollton for his son, Charles Carroll of Homewood, still stand and are open to the public. In addition, the Carroll Family papers constitute a collection of over seven thousand documents.

Given the extensive array of material available to those interested in the Carroll family, their history hardly seems an appropriate subject for a volume concerned with "unlocking secrets" and discovering a "hidden heritage." Nevertheless, the scholars charged with making the papers and houses accessible to the public have confronted the need for other pieces of evidence to help them fully understand and interpret their domain.

For Dr. Ronald Hoffman, editor of the Charles Carroll of Carrollton Papers, one challenge has been to achieve an understanding of the *mentalité* of the founder of the family fortunes, Charles Carroll the Settler. "The biography of the family . . . is set in Ireland and England as well as Maryland during the period from 1660 to 1782. It begins with the first Carroll to emigrate to Maryland, Charles Carroll the Settler, the grandfather of Charles Carroll of Carrollton. Yet, only *one* of his personal letters has survived, and a few other documents pertaining to his official activities. From the latter it is evident that understanding the Settler is absolutely critical to the family's story since it was he who laid down the base of the Carroll fortune, while at the same time challenging Maryland officialdom in a manner that eventually brought about the legislation which deprived him and his fellow Roman Catholics of their rights to hold office, to vote, to practice law, to give their children Catholic educations, and to practice their religion publicly. But how are we to find out about him—about what made him 'tick'—when there are scarcely any letters at all?

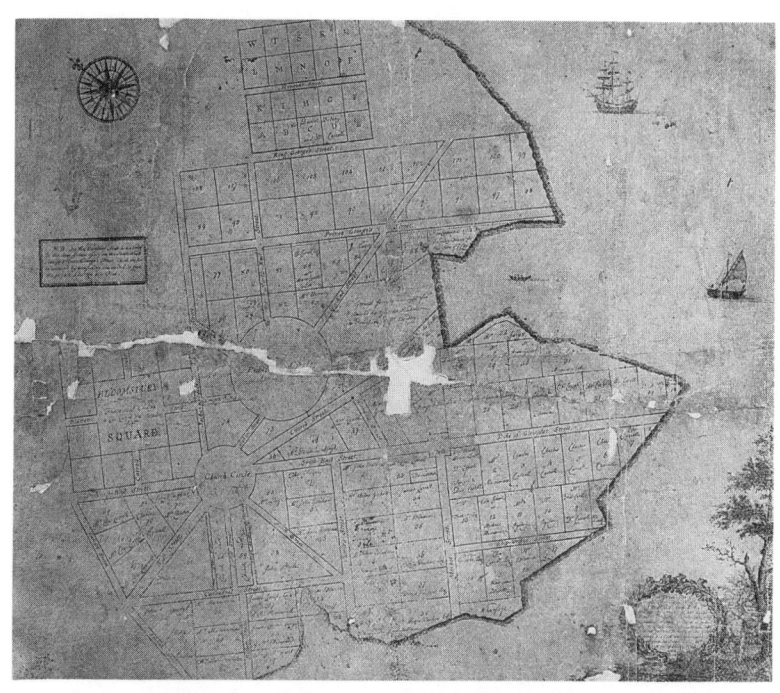

*This version of the 1718 Stoddert plat of Annapolis visually demonstrates Charles Carroll the Settler's pursuit of wealth. Carroll owned twenty-four lots in town, including most of those in the southeastern part of the city.*

"This is where the creative use of 'unusual sources' becomes so important. By using such techniques, it was possible to draw a vivid portrait. From land records—warrants, surveys, patents, and rent rolls—I recreated the process by which the Settler built his landed fortune. From court records I traced the evolution of his legal practice and his mortgage-holding and other banking activities. From inventories I established his style of life—which could hardly be called Spartan by the standards of his day. The variety and richness of the

*Despite his own thirty-year residence in Maryland and the birth of his sons in the colony, Charles Carroll the Settler still considered the family's Irish heritage important, illustrated here by a letter to sons Charles and Daniel, with its instructions to identify themselves as "Marylando-Hibernus." The physical landscape of the Doughoregan Valley in Ireland provided an unusual clue in the quest to understand the forces that inspired and motivated Charles Carroll the Settler.*

Settler's wearing apparel, the size of his house, and its elaborate furnishings indicate even more dramatically than the value of his estate the kind of presence he projected in Annapolis and provincial society. From the records of the proceedings of the Maryland legislature I was able to discover the high drama of this extraordinary man's bid to make himself the most powerful man in the province.

"Finally, from that one personal letter, together with recollections penned by his son and grandson, I was able to make the critical link between his Irish heritage and his Maryland career and to perceive the source of the emotional intensity that drove him until his death in 1720. In this instance, there were two vital pieces of evidence. First, the Settler's instructions to his son Charles Carroll of Annapolis in 1718 in that surviving personal letter, demanding that in defending his thesis at Douai, 'I would have you style yourself "Marylando-Hibernus,"' although he [the Settler] had been in Maryland for thirty years. Second, his son's recollection that when the Settler entered Maryland in 1688, he brought with him 'a little Irish Manuscript Book' containing the 'Genealogies of the O'Carrolls'—a document that remains in the family's possession today and which traces the Carrolls' roots to the beginning of the Gaelic past and well before."

The importance of their Irish heritage to the early Carrolls reveals itself also in the names that they gave to their lands in Maryland. Thus, the Irish landscape provided vital clues for reconstructing the values that motivated the Settler and his children. Dr. Hoffman and his staff explored that landscape during a visit to the Slieve Bloom mountains, the ancient home of the

O'Carroll chieftains, accompanied by a local resident, Paddy Heaney. "What we discovered on Mr. Heaney's tour was that many of the place names used by the Carrolls to designate their properties in Maryland originated in the hills and valleys where their forebears had fought against the incursions of the English during the sixteenth and seventeenth centuries.

"The most spectacular discovery occurred quite by accident. Charles Carroll of Carrollton's family called their dwelling plantation Doughoregan Manor. The conventional wisdom contained in a popular Carroll biography states that in Gaelic, Doughoregan means 'house of kings.' When I mentioned this to Mr. Heaney, he was quite puzzled and quickly corrected our misimpression by informing us that in Gaelic the name means 'the black fields of Regan.' Now it was our turn to be mystified—why, we asked, would the Carrolls name their principal seat 'the black fields of Regan'? Mr. Heaney didn't know, but said if we wished, he would be happy to show us the Doughoregan Valley. Since none of us knew such a valley existed, we were pleased to accept his offer. We drove up to it, high in the mountains, and when he pointed it out to us, we intuitively grasped why Carroll's grandfather, an ambitious man driven out of his country by forces beyond his control, might wish to carry with him the name of a magnificent valley as a reminder of the past and an embodiment of the future he wished to achieve in the new world."

Susan Tripp, Director of University Collections for the Johns Hopkins University, faced a different challenge when the University decided to restore Homewood House, located on its Baltimore campus, as a historic house museum. The home had been used over the years as student housing, as a faculty club, and most recently as offices for the deans. Now the University wished to return the building to its appearance during the early years of the nineteenth century when Charles Carroll of Homewood and his family lived there. Mrs. Tripp and her staff combined the insights provided by a variety of sources to restore the architectural structure of the house, furnish its interior, and interpret its usage by the family.

Archaeology of remains preserved underground allowed the project staff to "tie up a number of loose ends." For example, a question concerning the location of the privy—did it remain in its original site?—was answered when excavation around the base determined that the building had never been moved and therefore had been especially designed for its present location. Archaeology also recovered a considerable amount of Chinese export porcelain. "We had expected to find porcelain fragments but were gratified to find so much. These and other recovered ceramics provided clues to the kinds of items that were used in the house and the way the kitchen should be set up."

"As important to us as archaeology under the ground was the archaeology we pursued above the ground." When the deans moved out in 1982, the University Collections staff confronted an empty house. "What do you do with an empty house? It's a very daunting prospect. You don't want to rush in and paint; you don't want to make mistakes. We took out all of the modern carpeting, we took out all the drop ceilings, but we were still left with the question of not wanting to ruin any of the evidence that was in the house." As a first step, the University engaged an outside firm to prepare a historic structures report. "They went through the house on the exterior and the interior, noting what was original and what was a restoration feature, and did the paint analysis. Then they made a list of priorities for us to follow."

Historic photographs permitted restoration to their original form of a number of architectural features. When restoration of the house began in 1982, the north porch wall was completely filled in with brick but a photograph taken in 1892 showed the lintel of a window. "We studied the photograph and decided to put the window back. Knowing that there had been a window, we broke through from inside the house and found the additional brick used to fill in the windows originally designed to let light into the cellar area. We also were able to restore the balustrade on the south porch, which had been removed in 1930, by using evidence provided by early photographs. We obtained glass slides from Gilman School, dating from the years when they rented Homewood from the Wyman family. An 1899 photograph of a group of school boys on the porch preserved the perfect outlines of the balustrade."

Reconstruction of interior details relied upon several types of evidence. "For the interior we also studied old photographs. An 1892 photograph of the drawing room, for example, shows marbleizing on the baseboards. We recreated all of the marbleized baseboards and panels that the Carrolls knew when they lived in the house." A different form of evidence helped to return the kitchen to its original form. "Our kitchen is very large with high ceilings. It made sense to us that there would have been a built-in dresser, but we had to find the evidence for it. Because we knew that the plaster on the walls dated to a period later than the Carroll owner-

*This nineteenth-century photo of Gilman School boys on the front porch of the school shows only a small portion of the porch railing, but it was enough evidence to allow restoration of the porch to its original form.*

*The outlines, or ghosting, of the original kitchen shelving supplied the documentation needed to restore the shelves.*

ship, we removed the plaster and revealed the outline of our shelves. The wood butts straight up to the brick and the interaction of the two media—wood and brick—left a dark outline, or ghosting. We rebuilt our shelving on those lines."

Careful study of the present structure documented changes made to the house by the Carrolls and subsequent owners. For example, "a closet on the righthand side of the kitchen did not show up in any of the old drawings. When we took a careful look at it, it proved to be a doorway, cut into the kitchen after the Carrolls determined that a door between the kitchen and the adjoining housekeeper's room made the kitchen and service area a much easier place in which to function. This arrangement, which we restored, suits early nineteenth-century domestic economy practices, when the best dishes were kept with the housekeeper in her room and had to be carried there from the kitchen."

After returning the architecture of the house to its original form, restoration turned next to furnishing the house in an accurate manner. To draw up a furnishing plan, "we used Carroll family papers and inventories, all the Carroll letters, and Charles Carroll of Carrollton's orders to his agent in London" to authenticate the furnishings. Reproduction of the appropriate items often involved both detective work and luck. For example, "we knew that the family bought Brussels carpets. Through the National Trust in England we obtained access to 'point papers,' that is, papers prepared for the carpet weavers to allow them to set up the looms with the correct patterns. The drawing room carpet reproduces a design from 1803 that is signed and dated on the back of the point paper. The manufacturer has reissued the carpet after all these years."

Once a historic house has been restored as a museum site, its staff must create and implement a plan for its interpretation. The building must communicate something of its history and that of its owners to the visiting public. Devising an interpretation plan that engages the visitor, imparts information, and creates an enthusiasm for learning is a challenge continually faced by curators. Nor is it a static process that can be done once and then left in place for decades. The discovery of new sources of information and the focus on new questions and topics of concern require periodic reevaluation and reinterpretation.

The staff of the Carroll Mansion, part of the Baltimore City Life Museums, has recently engaged in such a process of reevaluation and reinterpretation for the house where Charles Carroll of Carrollton (father-in-law of its owner, Richard Caton) spent his winters from 1820 until his death in 1832. According to Barry Kessler, formerly Decorative Arts Curator, "the historic house museum is a curious hybrid beast. It showcases antique furnishings in a recreated setting designed to teach the public and schoolchildren about the history of craftsmanship and industry, about life and society in the past, and also about specific individuals and events. The Carroll Mansion juggles all these roles, and has done so since its inception. Early attempts to provide furnishings based on Carroll's inventory and on pictorial evidence were hampered by limited funds and a minimal collection, but the curators nevertheless created an elegant environment that spoke generally of the level of luxury consumption and space usage in a wealthy home of the period.

"Recently, heavy use, deferred maintenance, and increased attention derived from two very popular museum sites adjoining us built up enormous pressure for our staff to focus our efforts on the Carroll Mansion, and thus provided an opportunity significantly to improve its authenticity. Grant funding obtained in 1987 supported a project of object conservation, room improvements, and new visitor services for the Mansion. As research moved forward, we immediately realized that we faced a pair of problems: a paucity of evidence about the house itself and a corresponding abundance of evidence relating to Charles Carroll and his family. This imbalance, although awkward, would shift the focus away from the furnishings and toward an interpretation of Charles Carroll himself. The challenge was to forge from a rambling set of period rooms an effective tool for teaching the story of this Maryland patriot."

The project staff settled on a very basic message for the house: "This is how the last surviving signer of the Declaration of Independence spent the last years of his life. We would expound upon this message in every component of the refurbishing project: in the room settings, in a panel exhibit, and in self-guided tour books, as well as docent-led tours. A single key theme would run through the interpretation: the interaction between Charles Carroll and the numerous visitors who came to the house to see him."

Making the preliminary decisions about which rooms to interpret and how to furnish and paint those rooms left the more challenging task of then making the rooms speak to visitors. "Each of the exhibit rooms in the Mansion could tell a key piece of our story. But how could we give words to these furnished rooms so that they could communicate with the visitor? How could we people the rooms, rather than simply furnish them?

The exhibit we developed for the house brings the world of the Carroll household directly to the public through pertinent graphic and verbal historical evidence. The most important such sources are *portraits* of Charles Carroll, his family, and associates; *illustrations* of places central to Carroll's life; a few *genre scenes* showing period interiors; *original objects* belonging to Carroll and his family; and numerous *quotations* from diaries, travel accounts, and Carroll family letters.

"We used portraits extensively in the exhibition for their power to convey character and ambience. The image of Carroll that we used in the entry is his most public one—the posthumous portrait commissioned by the State of Maryland for the State House in 1832. Other portraits, by a variety of artists, appear on panels in various rooms to give a sense of how different artists viewed Carroll. In fact, the William Hubard portrait shown in the library panel was the starting point of a complete reinstallation of the room. We copied the color of the floorcloth and the cut and material of the slipcover on the chair directly from the picture.

"Direct quotations from early nineteenth-century visitors are perhaps the most important component of this exhibit, because they allow contemporary visitors to walk in the footsteps and see with the eyes of their predecessors 160 years ago. The experience of these visitors, who came, just as ours do today, to gain a first-hand, tangible knowledge of history by meeting Charles Carroll, are a most relevant source. These quotations consisted mostly of descriptions of the aged 'Relic of the Revolution,' his houses and family, and narratives of visits with them, Carroll's death, and his business activities.

*This portrait of the elderly Charles Carroll of Carrollton allows contemporary visitors to Carroll Mansion to share the experience of early nineteenth-century visitors who came to see the last living signer of the Declaration of Independence. At the same time, the portrait supplied the basis for the reinstallation of one room of the Carroll home.*

"One lucky find was a letter detailing the menu at a dinner at the Catons, although it probably took place after Charles Carroll's death, quoted in full on the panel in the dining room. We commissioned plastic food based on this letter and used a mass of evidence about dining customs of the wealthy to represent with reasonable accuracy the dining arrangements of the prosperous table.

"Our sources included the famous illustration of *The Dinner Party* by Henry Sargent and the 1827 butler's guide, *The House Servant's Directory*, by Robert Roberts." Once a ceramics expert identified the salad bowl now placed in the center of the table, for example, Roberts clarified its original usage. He directed that it be placed between the branches of the candelabra. "He also says to put a silver waiter under it, 'so as to raise [it] more majestically,' but unfortunately, our collection does not contain a waiter." Knowing what should be included on the table, however, provides guidance for the curators as they continue building the museum's collection.

"Finally, consider the most and least obvious pieces of evidence we chose to display. The Declaration of Independence is the most famous document in our national history, but we felt it was worth putting up on the wall

*Curators used this ca. 1821 painting by Henry Sargent of a dinner party as one of several sources that guided their interpretation of the Carroll dining room.*

> *Negroes*
>
> The following slaves belonging to the deceased at the time of his death are said to have resided in and were employed at the house of Richard Caton in the City of Baltimore or at the farm called Brookland Wood near the City of Baltimore on the 2nd September 1825 and shewn to the Appraisers on the 15th & 22nd April 1833.—
>
> | | | |
> |---|---|---|
> | Luke | 50 years of age | 250.— |
> | William (blind in one eye) | 55 " " | 100.— |
> | Richard | 36 " " | 200.— |
> | Polly | 60 " " | 40.— |
> | Sarah (daughter of Polly) | 35 " " | 200.— |
> | Katy | 50 " " | 80.— |
> | Nelly | 40 " " | 250.— |
> | Ellen (grand-child of old Henny) | 25 " " | 250.— |
> | Henry Hart (grand-child of old Henny) | 23 " " | 300.— |
> | William (Toney's son) | 25 " " | 300.— |
> | Sally (Charles's daughter) | 20 " " | 200.— |
> | Kitty (Ben's daughter) | 20 " " | 200.— |
> | Ellen (Harry Hart's daughter) | 3 " " | 250.— |
> | | | 2620 |

When Charles Carroll of Carrollton died, an inventory of his estate listed his possessions and their value, including those of his slaves who worked as domestic servants in the Baltimore home. Although the document supplies limited information about these members of the household—names, ages, infirmities, and some kinship ties—it nonetheless provides the only surviving record of their existence.

as a reference point. By contrast, information about the lives of domestic servants in the city homes of Baltimore's early nineteenth-century elite is extremely meager. We chose to display the section of Carroll's inventory which lists his slaves at Richard Caton's residence by name, age, and monetary value, along with Caton's complaint that the 'house was an asylum for [Carroll's] numerous family of colored people and in holliday times was rendered more like a barrack than a private residence.' "

Three different scholars, engaged in three different but related historical pursuits, have mined a variety of sources for nuggets of information that have allowed them to reconstruct portions of the past: the structure of a house, the furnishing and use of a room, the motivating force of an individual's career, the relationship between one man or one family and the broader society. They have, however, shared a common overarching purpose. Using both the obvious and the unusual clues, each has sought to understand as fully as possible his or her particular sphere of the Carroll story in order to convey that knowledge to the general public—to inform, to educate, to inspire, to enrich—whether the medium is a biography or a historic house.

# *Clues to the Past*

Anyone seeking to unlock the secrets of time confronts a vast array of potentially useful pieces of evidence.* He or she might choose to examine the assorted public records associated with an individual's death: a will, an inventory, the administrator's or guardian's bond or account, a list of debts collected, or the accounting of sales of the decedent's property. Visual images might provide different insights, whether from maps and charts, photographs, or paintings and drawings. Historical archaeologists examine sherds of pottery, frag-

---

*Scholars who participated in the "Unlocking the Secrets of Time" conference were asked to describe and evaluate different kinds of evidence with reference to particular places or specific social groups. Although their comments may, therefore, be directed toward the usefulness of census records for studying cannery workers or the insights that newspapers provide into the experiences of urban blacks, these and other sources can be used in the same ways to explore the histories of many different communities.

ments of bone, glass, and metal, stains left in the soil, and brick and stone building remains. Newspaper stories reveal contemporary perceptions of current events, but the columns of advertising have their own stories to tell. Oral histories, parish records, assessment books, census rolls, immigration passenger lists: all can supply the various bits of evidence that together solve a historical puzzle—or at least suggest an answer.

Susan Tripp has already commented upon the use of archaeological evidence to confirm the original location of one extant building in the Homewood complex. Dr. Henry Miller, Director of Research at Historic St. Mary's City, and his staff used archaeology to uncover the street plan and building sites of a vanished town.

According to Miller, we need to supplement the incomplete written record with another record, the material record or archaeological remains. "Archaeological sites," he observes, "are essentially a unique manuscript of the past. The site is basically made up of several components: features, something like brickwork or lines of stones, analogous to the pages of a manuscript; and sentences, the artifacts that are so valuable to date and to figure out what happened in an archaeological location.

"What about the evidence we get out of the archaeological record? We very seldom find specific names or specific dates. We're more generalized; we can look at changes over time and at broad social trends. Another limitation is that the evidence is woefully incomplete. Much of what people used in daily life has not survived. We have to read around the edges and piece together a puzzle to figure out what is really left. But there is an advantage: the record that's out there in the ground is incredibly democratic. Everyone, rich, poor, black, white, male, and female, leaves the record in the ground for us. One other advantage: it's not intentionally biased. We may misinterpret the record but it doesn't lie to us.

"Facts—objects recovered in excavations—only become evidence when we ask questions of them. Things that we never thought of as evidence before suddenly become radically significant when we ask the right questions. At St. Mary's City, we have been looking for years at the beginning of Maryland. St. Mary's, probably the best preserved seventeenth-century town site in America, became fossilized at the end of the seventeenth century, thereby preserving information about how Europeans and Africans changed when they came to the New World, how they created a new society, and how they adapted to the wilderness of Maryland." Among the questions asked by St. Mary's research staff: What was the first city in Maryland like?

"Working from the limited documentary evidence, we put together a map of how the city possibly looked, as a haphazard, organic village. But was this correct? When we excavated in the crossroads area, where the main roads came together, by plowing and surface collecting the artifacts, we found no seventeenth-century artifacts. We continued looking and eventually found seventeenth-century artifacts clustered elsewhere, near an 1840s plantation house. We scattered squares randomly in the area looking for traces of a fence line, a building, anything to locate the town. In square twelve, we found a corner of a brick footing, possible a foundation. We continued to dig and the building became larger and larger, but what was it? According to the

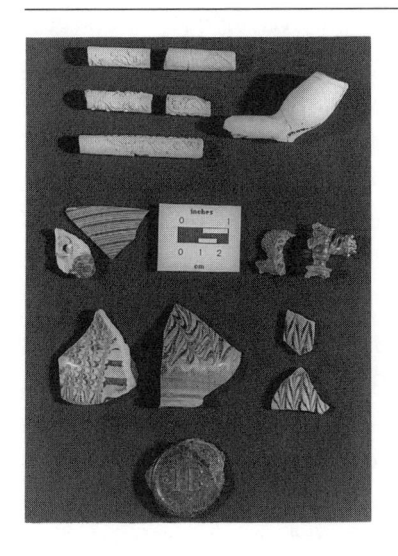

*These fragments of tobacco pipes, glass, ceramics, and a bottle seal—seemingly mute bits of clay and sand—told St. Mary's City archaeologists that they had uncovered the remains of one of the first capital's most important seventeenth-century buildings.*

documents no building should have existed in that location."

To identify the building, the archaeologists needed to determine when the building was constructed and how long it stood. A variety of artifacts provided the clues they needed. "The tobacco pipes, with their varying decorations, were made in the Netherlands and date from the 1630s, 1640s, and 1650s, so we know the building had to have been constructed during the early years of settlement. Other artifacts dated from a later period. Fragments of table glass probably came from Venice or the Netherlands, elegant tableware made in the 1660s and 1670s. Ceramics provide another invaluable dating tool. Staffordshire slipware was not made until about 1675 or 1680, so the building had been occupied until the end of the century. Then a student turned up a clue that was very important, a glass bottle seal with the initials 'JB.' Here the history and the ar-

*Clues to the Past*

chaeology come together. John Baker was the largest tavernkeeper in the eighteenth century, leasing the home of the first governor, Leonard Calvert, as his tavern. This building was constructed about 1636 and stood until the end of the century. We also knew the width of the Calvert lot, 148', a dimension that matched the length of the fence line—150'—surrounding the house.

"All these pieces of information merged to tell us that we had found the 'Country's House,' the home of the first governor that later became the state house of Maryland. This was the structure that was at the core of the city; everything else was built around it. With that clue in hand, we continued the excavations elsewhere, looking for and finding the other buildings that we knew from the documents should have been there: Cordea's Hope, a lawyer's office, and the remains of Smith's tavern. Using all of our evidence, we created a new map, the first reasonably accurate map of St. Mary's City.

"We could now answer the question of what the first capital was really like. Was it the haphazard community shown in the first map? To answer that question, we looked for measurements. Rather than the irregular pattern we expected, we found a square at the center of town, equidistant placement of the state house and the great brick chapel on the west and east sides of the town, and symmetric placement of the prison, school, and two entrance ways to the town. What we have is a very unusual layout for a seventeenth-century city, laid out according to the most sophisticated ideas of urban planning available at the time, the Baroque concept coming from Italy. I believe now that Lord Baltimore was trying to make the capital of his colony a much more sophisticated and impressive place than we had ever thought. This is a good example of how archaeological evidence can change our notions of the past, for there is no trace in the historical record of this planning, but the evidence on the ground is indisputable."

While researchers at St. Mary's City used traditional archaeological techniques to explore the past, other scholars at Salisbury State University are using sophisticated modern technology both to uncover hidden evidence and to preserve the present for future researchers. Their project looks at the material or archaeological resources of the historic and prehistoric past of Maryland and particularly of the Eastern Shore. With funding since 1987 from the National Oceanic and Atmospheric Administration, the Environmental Protection Agency, the Department of Agriculture, and other federal and state agencies, they have developed a computer system for integrating various types of geographically grounded resources.

According to Dr. Peter Lade, development of the computer project was prompted by "the knowledge that in the next few years an increasing amount of diverse data would need to be considered to make appropriate decisions for the protection of both natural and cultural resources, and the realization that manual handling of large amounts of data would not be practical. It is apparent to all of us that the amount of data that we're asked to interpret or analyze has increased in a staggering fashion. The purpose of the project at Salisbury is to provide a means by which we can take detailed information on the location, extent, and values of different types of natural and cultural resources and interactively

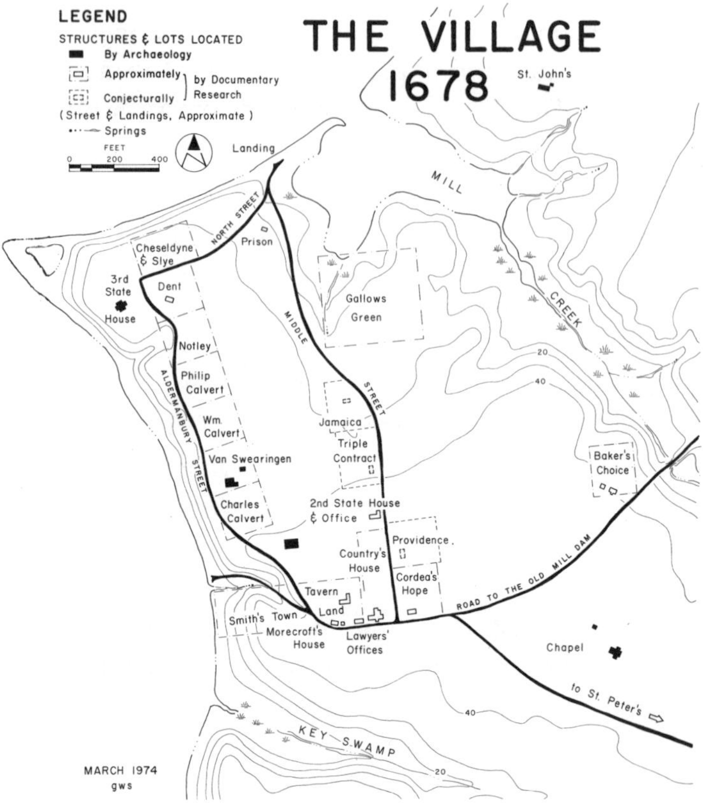
LEGEND
STRUCTURES & LOTS LOCATED
By Archaeology
Approximately
Conjecturally
by Documentary Research
(Street & Landings, Approximate)
Springs
FEET
0 200 400
THE VILLAGE
1678
St. John's
Landing
MILL
CREEK
NORTH STREET
Prison
Cheseldyne & Slye
3rd State House
Dent
Gallows Green
MIDDLE STREET
Notley
Philip Calvert
ALDERMANBURY STREET
Wm. Calvert
Jamaica
Triple Contract
Van Swearingen
Baker's Choice
Charles Calvert
2nd State House & Office
Providence
Country's House
Cordea's Hope
ROAD TO THE OLD MILL DAM
Tavern Land
Smith's Town
Morecroft's House
Lawyers' Offices
Chapel
to St. Peter's
KEY SWAMP
20
40
MARCH 1974
gws

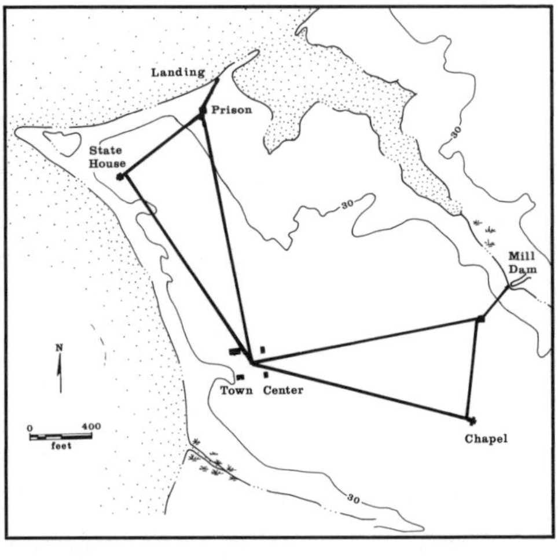
Landing
Prison
State House
Mill Dam
N
0 400
feet
Town Center
Chapel
30

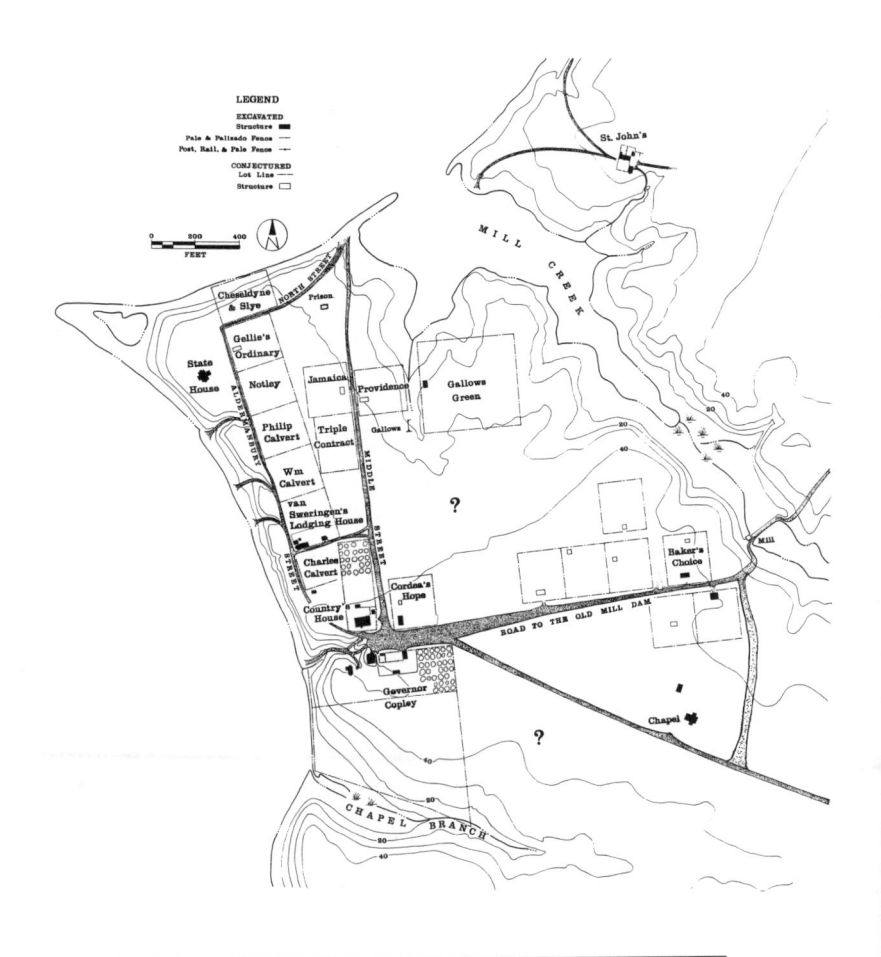

*The plan on the left, based on the documentary evidence, represents the town that archaeologists expected to find: an unplanned, haphazard, organic village. The plan on the right depicts the actual town as revealed through archaeological excavation: a formal, planned settlement laid out according to Baroque principles of urban design with the most important public buildings geometrically related.*

manipulate them by computer. We can address questions of why these resources might be important now, why they might be important to preserve for the future, and how they have changed or been lost in the past. By expanding the original computer capabilities that existed as part of traditional geographic information systems from purely image processing to include overlays, we enable archaeological and historical sites, soil layers, land use patterns, historical property maps, and similar kinds of data to be brought into a computerized system.

"At Salisbury, for example, we monitor near-shore areas for underwater archaeological resources. In this case, we know that image-processing techniques can evaluate the condition of sediments and erosional patterns, the effects of sea level rise, and other factors that determine whether or not archaeological sites and early historic sites might have been present and also whether or not they might have been preserved. We know that many of the archaeological sites from contact and precontact periods are now no longer on land but rather lost. Reconstruction of that loss through the overlay of other kinds of data sources using a computer at least allows us to determine where it is most profitable to look for early settlements.

"Perhaps more dramatic is the use of satellite data, looking from a distance of over four hundred miles, with a remarkable degree of resolution. Through a variety of different bands, it is possible to bring out features that represent not only land use and land cover but that may also indicate by their exception the presence of archaeological sites and the ecological conditions under which they originally occurred. The impressive amount of detail revealed through satellite data indicates their potential not only for monitoring and maintaining our record of historic and archaeological sites, but also for maintaining a record of current development that would allow us to document the present for the future as well as to analyze data from the past."

The State of Maryland, through the Maryland Historical Trust, has its own project in underwater archaeology. Paul Hundley, the Trust's underwater archaeologist, defines marine archaeology as the study of "past life on or related to the sea, whether it is how ships were built, what ports they visited, or the way of life of the people who sailed them. Artifacts recovered from submerged sites are not studied simply for themselves, but for the insight they provide about the people who made and used them. The ultimate goal is the better understanding of human behavior and culture. Maryland with its rich maritime heritage offers the maritime archaeologist a vast resource to study."

Marine archaeology involves the use of its own specialized technology to expand the process of recovery and analysis. In 1979, Maryland undertook "the first scientific study of submerged archaeological resources in the survey of the Barney flotilla, a group of vessels scuttled during the war of 1812. Working in near-zero visibility, divers were able to measure and draw the construction features of one fleet vessel. A high-resolution, low-light camera was used as an experimental method of recording parts of the vessel. For the survey of the *Henrietta Bach,* a nineteenth-century schooner which lies in St. Leonard's Creek, an underwater video camera mounted on a remotely operated vehicle was used to record the hull remains and guide the use of the ROV's hand-like manipulator. Later divers worked with a sonic high-accuracy ranking and positioning system to map the timbers on the bottom. Using this technology, two divers were able to do in hours what it would have taken a team of people weeks to do by hand."

Not all discoveries are the product of modern technology, however. "Last fall a very exciting find was unearthed with equipment not normally used in archaeological excavation—an oyster dredge. A waterman called to report finding a strange piece of pottery. This piece, dated 1593, is believed to be the oldest dated piece of ceramics yet found in the United States. The Maryland Historical Trust will be investigating this site, which comes from near Kent Island and may be associated with William Claiborne's settlement or an even earlier exploration of the Chesapeake."

Peter Lade's work involves the combination of photographic images with other mapped data to identify sites of archaeological significance. Gilbert Gude, historian of a different water-related region—the towns along the Potomac River—uses photographs in combination with another research technique, oral history. "Photographs are great stimulators in expanding local histories. When I was researching the history of the North Branch of the Potomac, I was looking for any material on Kempton, just several miles from the beginning of the Potomac at the Fairfax Stone. Today Kempton is practically a ghost town, with only seven houses where miners' widows, children, and grandchildren live. Because Kempton had been a company coal town, I thought I might find at least one picture from the Farm Security Administration collections at the Library of Congress taken somewhere in the western Maryland or West Virginia region. I struck a gold mine: seventy-nine pictures taken in 1939 in Kempton. Xerox copies, shown to citizens and former residents of the town, stirred lots of memories."

When used as historic resources in their own right, photographs provide invaluable insights but must be used with care, as historian Linda Shopes notes. "Photographs are probably one of the most difficult sources to decode for those more familiar with words than pictures. For pictures are not simply a faithful record of what is or was—they are highly subjective documents and to begin to interpret them we must ask who took the photograph, what subject was chosen (and therefore what was *not* photographed), and for what purpose the picture was taken.

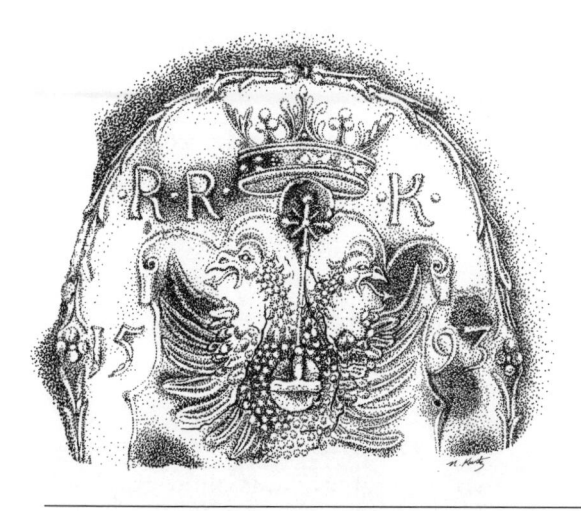

*This fragment of sixteenth-century pottery is unusual because it was recovered by an oyster tong, not an ordinary research tool. More significant, however, are the questions raised by its presence in an area not formally settled until the second quarter of the seventeenth century.*

*This photograph of the company doctor leaving the home of a sick miner captures both the physical and the social landscape of Kempton.*

"For example, in July of 1909 the social photographer Lewis Hine was lugging his tripod, glass plates, and box camera around the Fells Point cannery district and the farms of Anne Arundel County photographing children at work. Two years later he was photographing some of these same children who had migrated with their families to the Gulf Coast for the winter to work in the oyster and shrimp packing plants there. Hine was employed by the National Child Labor Committee, an organization dedicated to the abolition of child labor.

*Photographer Lewis Hine captioned his photo of the interior of the S. J. Ferrand Packing Company in Baltimore: "Many tiny workers. Babies are held on the laps of workers, or stowed away in empty boxes." The field workers he described as "Mrs. Lessie and family (Polish). They all work in fields in Baltimore [actually Anne Arundel County] in summer and have worked at Biloxi, Mississippi for two years."*

From the point of view of the NCLC, child labor was a scourge upon the land, ruining health and closing off opportunities for education and hence a better life for the working-class children who worked in the mines and mills and factories and fields. Hine's photographs were thus intended as propaganda devices, designed to educate an unsuspecting middle-class public to the existence of child labor.

"Hine was obviously trying to arouse the public's sympathy and pity for these children. Yet I have interviewed a number of people who had actually worked in the canneries and fields as children and they have an entirely different view of things. Many still feel proud to have helped their families out; they feel their mothers were teaching them necessary habits of hard work and family assistance. As one woman said to me indignantly, 'It didn't hurt us any.' And when I mentioned to another gentleman that some people thought it was bad for children to be working, he replied: 'I don't know who you've been talking to, but they must have had children who didn't like to work.' Many also recall the trip to the country as a vacation—of course the work was hard, hot, and bug-ridden, but there was also the pleasure of being in the open air. This perspective on child labor is not obvious looking at Hine's photographs, and indeed stands in opposition to their very intent."

Photographs provide one means of entry into the lives of groups within the population who may not have left extensive collections of letters or other written documents. Newspapers provide a similar point of access into the culture of those communities. In discussing sources for exploring the history of urban African Americans, museum director Steven Newsome began by observing that "traditionally, the exceptional person or event has been used as a point of reference in developing historical studies of societies or groups of people. In this manner, the society being studied has been approached with the cultural bias of the historian. The bias has largely been Eurocentric, and has made the historian use primarily records easily accessible and available in the mainstream institutions. The result: short-sighted views of African-American history, omissions in textbooks, gaps in educational curricula, and almost no representation in museums, special library collections, and archives. We're all aware of the larger projects that have helped to fill these gaps, that have made it very clear that African Americans have made lasting contributions to just about every area of human endeavor. But still, documenting the African-American experience is a big challenge.

"We need to provide information that allows a public interpretation of the African-American experience, particularly in the urban environment. The first important thing to remember is that it is, or should be, the community, not the scholar, that defines what is significant or important. Secondly, we should all be aware that the documentation which supports that importance cannot always be found in institutions outside of that community. While some material may indeed be located in historical societies, archives, and mainstream libraries, the bulk of both material culture and documentation can still be found in the African-American community: in trunks, in basements, in attics, in church records, organizational records, black newspapers, and—very importantly—in the memories of elders in the community.

"Perhaps the most significant advantage of doing research on the black experience in an urban environment, particularly in the nineteenth and twentieth centuries, is the likelihood of the existence of a black newspaper. The Baltimore *Afro-American,* for example, is now in its ninety-eighth year. Black newspapers could, and should, be used as an index to the black community, not just as a newspaper. This index provides insight into a black perspective on major news issues, their reporting and editorials. They consistently provide access to information on the black churches and their activities, commentary about black political leaders, coverage of the black social scene, and a directory of black businesses. In essence, the definition of the community and access to that community come as a result of using the newspaper. It is the use of these resources in combination with materials that are available in mainstream institutions that allows us to get a fuller picture of the community."

Newspapers supply a valuable resource for the study of working-class white communities as well. Linda Shopes has "found it useful to mine newspapers for information about the more active, public roles working-class people have taken to shape their lives. For example, reading the standard in-house account of the canning industry in Baltimore—written by the men who ran the industry—I learned that they experienced considerable conflict with hand canmakers, skilled craftworkers who resisted efforts to mechanize their trade. But this was simply noted in a lengthy encomium to technological progress. To find out more about these canmakers, I scanned the local news section of the Baltimore morning *Sun* from the late 1860s through the 1890s and *The Critic,* a local labor paper, during the late

*Newspapers such as Baltimore's 1915* The Commonwealth *offer rare windows into the past religious, social, and economic experiences of the African-American community.*

1880s and early 90s. I discovered that this group of workers, some seven hundred strong, were among the earliest and most powerful local of the Knights of Labor in Baltimore; that they engaged in a protracted, twenty-year militant struggle to control their skills, including almost annual strikes and the organization of a national boycott of machine-made cans; and that they led the local labor movement in the late nineteenth century, heading a demonstration of some fifteen thousand

48   Unlocking the Secrets of Time

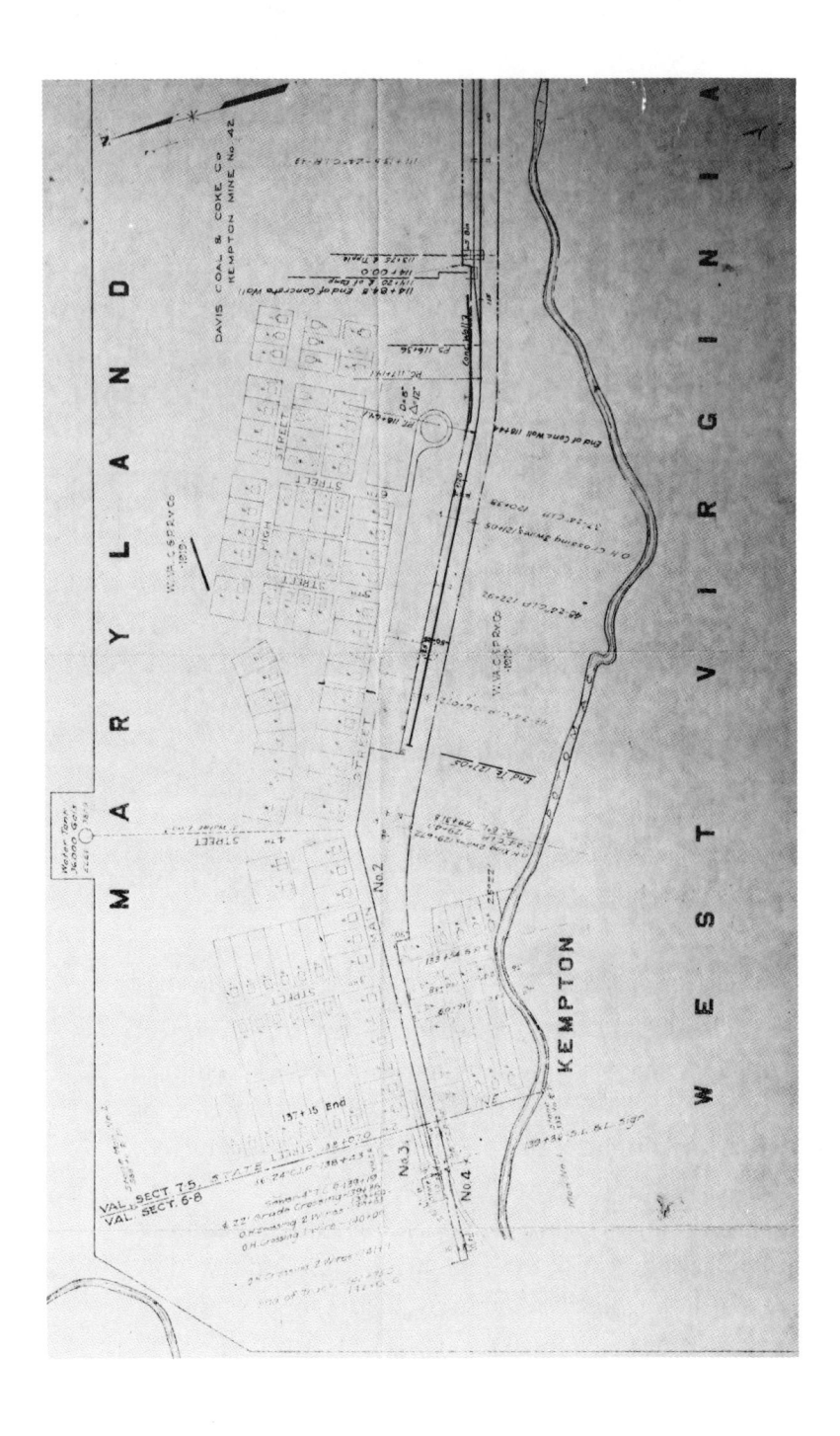

working Baltimoreans on May Day, 1886 in support of the eight-hour day.

"Information about dozens of other topics relevant to working class life can be found by reading the newspapers. Ward politics are faithfully recorded, including the political debates that took place in working-class clubs. Church services and sermons are reported; likewise, the meetings of social clubs and other organizations. All of this information can be used to develop a picture of working-class men and women creating a complex social identity and social life for themselves."

Both Shopes and Gude have employed oral history as part of their research into communities as diverse as western Maryland miners and Baltimore cannery workers. For Gude, maps provided another means of stimulating the memories of those he interviewed. A 1919 right-of-way and track map of Kempton, for example, served as such a memory aid. "The town, established in 1913, at its largest was a community of 116 houses. The engineering map showed all of the houses, street names, and even the location, capacity, and elevation of the water tower. The enlarged town segment proved invaluable in getting present and former inhabitants of the town to help me build a good picture of the sociology and culture of the community. As soon as I unrolled the map and the people oriented themselves to it, it was like turning on a faucet—out the recollections would flow. If there were two or more oldtimers

---

*Town maps, such as this 1919 map of Kempton, can be used in oral history interviews to stimulate the memories of those being interviewed.*

*Clues to the Past*  49

looking at the map, they stimulated each other to more and more remembrances and also checked each other as to accuracy. I soon knew where the Kempton shakers and movers lived: the mine officials, the ladies' aid and women's Christian service's officers, even some members of the little company town's historical society. For example, the principal of the school lived next to the Potomac, in what I was assured was the well-kept part of town; the doctor had his office in one end of the school house on Main Street. The English lived on Main Street while immigrants from Eastern Europe and Italians lived on the back streets."

Gude warns that "when we use oral history we have to take into account the reliability of human memory as well as bias or prejudice." But by interviewing several people on the same subject or by having a group of people talk about a particular topic, correcting one another's memories, an accurate history can be constructed. "Always ask questions, never take things for granted, nor let preconceived notions be so stubborn as to exclude new information or data from your consideration."

Linda Shopes also notes the strengths and dangers of using oral history. "For a description of the more private aspects of working-class life, the everyday experiences of childhood and gender relations, for example, for a perspective of that life from the point of view of the participants, and for a record of working-class consciousness, the best single source, I think, is oral history. Working-class men and women, when approached by a skilled, sensitive, and thoughtful interviewer, can speak eloquently about the most intimate details of life and can provide an interpretation of the American past that belies accounts fashioned from more mainstream sources and by historians without much insight into the nature of class relations.

"For example, the exhibit at Tindeco Wharf, a former can factory now converted into condos along Baltimore's waterfront, tastefully displays the decorative cans produced by Tindeco and pridefully notes that the company was run by rather enlightened manufacturers—unlike many of the dingy and poorly lit factories in the area. Tindeco had lots of windows and even an interior courtyard to let in natural light. Yet when I remarked on this to a woman I was interviewing who had worked there, her comment was: 'I don't know about that—all I remember is clamping those damn Bayer aspirin tins for a lousy 25 cents an hour.'

"Much, of course, has been said about the evidentiary value of oral history—how accurate, after all, is memory some forty, fifty, or sixty years after an event. My own experience suggests that a well-prepared interviewer, grounded in the extant historical record, working hard to create an atmosphere of trust and expansiveness in an interview, and willing gently to challenge variant accounts, can do a great deal to create thoughtful recall. It's important, too, to interview a number of people within the group or community you're researching; evidence is cumulative, and one begins to get an ethnographic sense for the contours of daily life, for the culture, rather than one person's necessarily particular, individual experience. Of course, interviews contain factual inaccuracies, but their value is not so much as a record of fact—although they can be that—but as a record of consciousness, how people felt about their experience, how they understand their world and their place in it. And, despite certain common insights into the culture that interviews can provide, individual accounts and interpretations differ. But history, after all, isn't a simple, single truth that needs to be faithfully recovered; there are, indeed, many pasts, many different experiences and versions of those experiences, depending on the social position and point of view of the participants. Certainly unionization at Bethlehem Steel was experienced differently by management and labor, and differently yet again by union organizers and those they were trying to unionize."

Other scholars utilize documentary evidence to recreate community landscapes over time. Historian Lois Green Carr traced the process for Cecil County, beginning with a series of maps that capture the changes in the physical contours that have occurred over three centuries. A soil map, produced by the Soil Conservation Service in cooperation with the Maryland Department of Agriculture (similar maps are available for every county in Maryland), shows the distribution of soil types within the county. The map identifies areas suitable for agriculture and the crops that could be grown there to best advantage, woodland areas, and locations of mineral resources. Carr says, "Geological formations are reflected in the soil map. Stone, mostly granite, underlies the dark soils of the piedmont. Below the piedmont are the gravels, sands, and clays of the Atlantic coastal plain. Although Cecil has been largely an agricultural county, the granite quarries along the Susquehanna River are famous and helped support the town of Port Deposit. Iron was once mined near Elkton and attempts have been made to find gold. For a while in the nineteenth century the area along the boundary of Cecil County and Lancaster County in Pennsylvania was the source of almost all the chrome used the world over.

These formations and their minerals and soils are the foundation of the county landscape.

"Augustine Herrman made a map of Maryland for Lord Baltimore during the 1660s in return for a large land grant, Bohemia Manor, in what became Cecil County. The map, published in 1673, shows that the earliest settlement was confined to the excellent agricultural lands in the tidewater area east of the Elk River. A map of 1751, by Peter Jefferson and Joshua Fry, was the first to show the beginnings of a road system that remains today, plus several early villages. The next improvement in such information came in 1795, with the map by Dennis Griffith, which shows a more complex road system plus towns, forges, mills, and inns. Settlement information of this kind does not appear again until Simon Martenet's map of 1858, which gives great detail of the cultural landscape—not only roads, but railroads, canals, churches, grist and saw mills, textile mills, iron furnaces, and other enterprises, including farm houses. This map is also useful for its insets of Cecil towns. The early twentieth-century geological maps today are updated with detail obtainable from aerial photographs. All these materials offer a visual picture of continuity and change over time in the county landscape."

Other scholars stress the usefulness of studying a central institution to understand a community. According to Steven Newsome, "one of the primary institutions within the black community is the black church, or the black churches—it is not a monolith. The African-American church provides us not just the history of the church but of the community: births, marriages, baptisms, and deaths. The printed programs from the

*Simon Martenet's 1858 map of Cecil County, taken from an atlas of all Maryland counties, documents a wide range of man-made additions to the landscape: roads, towns, mills, stores, churches, schools, homes, and an array of similar features.*

church activities provide the names of church and community leaders, and supply basic information about community social structure. Let us not forget that since the late nineteenth century in particular, the African-American church has been the central institution providing not only spiritual guidance, but political, social, and economic guidance as well. It is the churches which responded when southern governments failed to desegregate the schools. Therefore, the African-American church acted as a school for its community. It is also the traditional source of leadership for the civil rights movement. The impact is so great, in terms of the church, that we can also see it in tangible sources as well. The structure of the civil rights marches, for example, is that of a church processional. That same structure, the structure of the black church, influenced so greatly the structure of any organization that emerged from the church that you will find the hierarchy of social and civic organizations reflecting the structure of the African-American church.

"The evidence that emerges from the African-American church includes printed programs, photographs, church objects, textiles such as robes and uniforms, and badges. We also have the intangibles: music, gospel music, spirituals, forms of music which have influenced just about every genre of American music today. It should also be understood that African-American churches had distinctions among themselves: there were affluent, middle-class, and poor churches. Thus, access to institutions allows the researcher to examine both racial and class distinctions at the same time.

"As we consider the twentieth-century urban experience among African Americans, it is important to re-

*Members of the Forest Hills Wesley Methodist Chapel congregation posed on the steps of the church about the time of the chapel's re-dedication in 1930. Some church records and memorabilia are on deposit at the Maryland State Archives; most are still retained by the individual congregations.*

member that the churches were affected by a major social movement: migration. There was both interstate and intrastate migration beginning around 1910, with its biggest impact between 1918 and 1940. This migration brought rural traditions to the city, particularly giving flavor to religious worship, cooking, and style of dress."

Other institutions played an important role in creating and sustaining a community. "It is also important to remember that this migration gave rise to organizations designed to assist new arrivals in adjustment to their new environment. No examination of black urban life after 1910 is complete without looking at the work of the NAACP or the Urban League and their respective publications. These organizations, in turn, gave rise to other self-improvement and benevolent societies aimed at making life in segregated society better. Going back to newspapers in urban areas, one finds evidence of what Constance Green called the "secret city," a separate black society, a separate black infrastructure, sometimes modeled after existing white institutions: cultural clubs, choral societies, instrumental groups, oratorical societies, and the like. As an example, Baltimore had in the 1920s a colored symphonic league. The records of Morgan State University, the University of Maryland–Eastern Shore, Bowie State University, and Coppin State provide excellent opportunities for documentation of the cultural manifestations of academic life: academic achievement, sports, and, very importantly, fraternities and sororities. These organizations are critical for understanding the African-American sense of ritual and performance."

Newsome argues that "it is important in going about the documentation and interpretation of black urban experience to understand that American racism caused the creation of a separate society. Even in situations such as Maryland, where there was a large population of free blacks, a separate society had to exist. Manifestations of that society, the material culture, still reside primarily in that community. It is important, then, to understand how these two communities intersected and interacted, particularly to begin to assess urban life in general. One of the problems that we find today, when we look at what city life has been like for everyone, is that many things have been omitted. The great homes have been restored, without any reference to the cooks, the caterers, the launderers, the delivery boys and girls. How then can that interpretation be complete without any pictures of the black folks who worked so hard to make life what it was? It can't be. How can the interpretation of plantation life be complete without the images of the African American? It just can't be. So we have to overcome these biases. What we are facing now is that no analysis of urban life can be done without analysis of the African-American experience. The understanding of the urban black experience becomes more and more critical to understanding our society at large. Different methodologies, including archaeology, are now beginning to look at black life for a fuller understanding of city life. The ordinary has become significant. The hidden has become present."

Both Henry Miller and Steven Newsome have observed that the archaeological record encompasses all groups within society. Probate records provide a second category of evidence that documents both rich and poor, both white and black. Single inventories detail the possessions of one individual while large samples reveal the contours of the larger community. For Ronald Hoffman, the inventory of Charles Carroll the Settler illuminated Carroll's style of life. "The variety and richness of the Settler's wearing apparel, the size of his house, and its elaborate furnishings indicate even more dramatically than the value of his estate the kind of presence he projected in Annapolis and provincial society. His wardrobe included eight suits, one of which was a splendid affair of 'fine Cloath trimmed with gold,' and five wigs among dozens of garments. His house contained eleven well-appointed rooms with not only such marks of gentility as featherbeds and chairs but also an array of refinements that signified a style of living virtually unequalled in Maryland at that period. There were portraits and pictures on the walls, looking glasses and clocks, plate and fine linen for genteel dining, separate utensils in the bed chamber for tea service, and a kitchen equipped for preparing meals of elegance and sophistication."

Historian Lorena Walsh, on the other hand, used inventories to look at resources of yeoman farmers (those

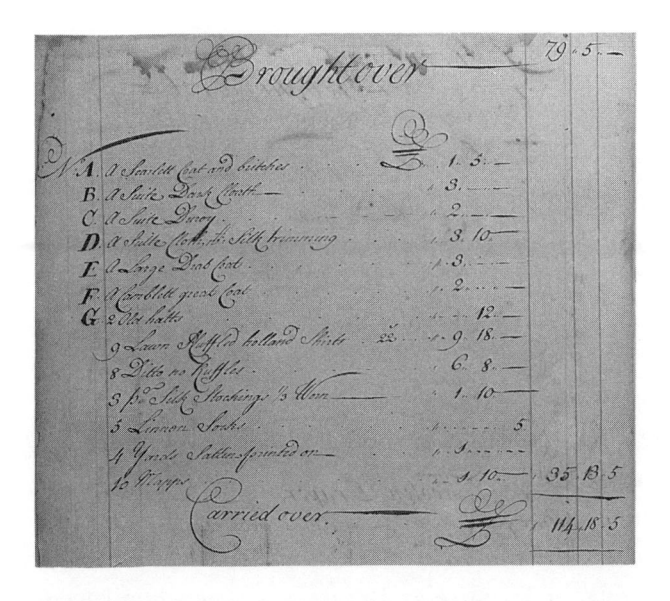

*This small section of Charles Carroll the Settler's inventory—with its notations of scarlet coats, silk-trimmed suits, ruffled shirts, and silk stockings—provides eloquent testimony to the wealth enjoyed by the Settler. At £115, the value of his clothing alone exceeded the total wealth of most of his contemporaries in the colony.*

who worked with their hands, whether tenants or small landowners) and the strategies they adopted to make the most of those resources. "When using probate inventories," Walsh warns, "some cautions are in order. Older, richer families are better represented in probate than younger, poorer ones. The distribution of wealth that inventories show is not that of the living population. Nonetheless, if we want to look at different strategies for making a living, we can arrange inventories into economic groups.

"If we add information from land records and wills, we can divide farmers according to their ownership of land and labor, starting at the bottom with tenants, then landowners with no servants or slaves, followed by somewhat better-off landowners who probably still worked in the fields but who employed a few bound laborers to supplement the family workers, and ending at the top with large planters with many unfree workers who themselves avoided manual labor. The information from inventories is broadly representative of the activities of these groups, even if it does not provide an accurate picture of the proportion of families who lived at these various levels. Analysis of inventories provides an overall picture that is consistent from one group to another. Tenant farmers and small planters always had access to the least amount of labor, had the least diversified mix of farming and craft equipment, and were most dependent on exchanging a cash crop—primarily tobacco—for other family needs.

"Wills offer a second source for studying the yeoman farmer, but because many small planters and most tenants did not make them, wills are less complete and even more biased towards richer farmers than are inven-

This account of the estate of Jacob Cramer of Frederick County lists first the assets belonging to the decedent and next the expenses paid by his administrator, including rents for the land Cramer leased from the proprietor. The balance remaining was divided among Cramer's widow and his nine children.

tories. For those who left them, however, wills can reveal the amount of land the family owned and its location, and the numbers and approximate ages of the children, the way the farmer chose to divide his assets among family members, cooperative arrangements for sharing use of orchards or tools, provisions for educating children, and some evidence as to whether the testator was literate, among other things.

"The accounts that were often, but not always, filed as an estate was settled are also important. In Maryland, many accounts record the crops produced in the year the farmer died. They also include expenses paid by the executor or administrator. Often the record of payments is not too revealing—only the amounts paid and the payee. But when the account includes the reason for the expense, we may learn whether the farmer owned or rented land, his religion if a funeral sermon was preached and the minister named, the merchants to whom he was indebted, and so forth."

For Lois Carr, "probate records offer a fascinating route into the daily life of people, especially before the U.S. Census began to provide details in 1850. In colonial Maryland the estate of anyone who left a will had to go through probate, a process that required an inventory of all movable assets that creditors and legatees might claim and that supposedly resulted in an account showing what debts were due and paid and the final balance of the estate. If there were no will, an heir or creditor could ask the court to act, with the same result. Many people already know the value of these records for family history. In recent years, historians have been discovering that these documents can tell about everyday existence in a period when most communication was

*This inventory of the property of Enos Mackdaniel of Calvert County stands in marked contrast to that of Charles Carroll. Mackdaniel's clothes, other than those in which he was buried, consisted only of a hat, coat, and worn vest. Mackdaniel grew only tobacco as a cash crop, lived in a sparsely furnished house, and owned few tools. His inventory is typical of those of poor planters in the seventeenth and early eighteenth centuries.*

unwritten. Inventories reveal how people earned their livings, the technology available, the spatial arrangements of their houses, something about their diet, how they prepared food, and what household furnishings they had.

"By comparing inventories, for example those of a rich man and a poor man from two periods—the last quarter

*Clues to the Past* 63

of the seventeenth century, at the beginning of settlement, and the 1770s, a century later—we can observe some of the changes taking place in the economy and society over that span. Both seventeenth-century inventories show tobacco crops but are without the plows that would make it practical to grow wheat on any scale. Both eighteenth-century inventories show plows and carts and contain references to wheat and other grains, but no tobacco. In both the earlier inventories, there is no equipment for home manufactures, such as spinning wheels or looms or shoemaking tools, nor is any craft represented except carpentry. There are also no sheep. By contrast, there are spinning wheels in the later households, and flax and sheep appear.

"If these inventories are typical, they tell us that seventeenth-century planters concentrated on tobacco, importing all their clothing and household equipment, which they purchased in return for their crop. Because they could not import housing or fencing, carpentry skills were needed and the tools were on hand to exercise it. By the 1770s, the whole basis of the Cecil economy had shifted from tobacco to grains and had diversified in other ways. Planters' wives were spinning wool and flax and there were surely weavers in the neighborhood to weave the yarn into clothing. There must also have been blacksmiths to maintain the plows and cartmakers and wheelwrights to provide equipment for hauling the grains from the fields. The economy was more diversified; planters and their families lived a more varied life than they had in the seventeenth century. Of course, we cannot infer much from four inventories alone. But if we look at large numbers over time, we can find evidence for such generalizations and determine when changes took place.

"Inventories tell us a variety of other things. One can discover the predominance of servants in the seventeenth century and follow the transformation of the bound labor force from servant to slave. This was a fundamental social change occurring at different rates across the colony, rates that can be measured through inventory entries. Also of great interest are household furnishings. The seventeenth-century households, whether rich or poor, are sparsely furnished. Nearly a century later, both rich and poor are living in more elaborately furnished houses and show signs of gentility in dining—table forks, drinking glasses, tea ware—that are missing in the seventeenth century. Thus through inventories we can follow changes across time in the standard of living and in social habits and attitudes.

"There are things of importance that inventories do not reveal. We can learn something about diet, but far from all we would like. Little food is mentioned. Perishables were never inventoried and the family of the deceased could omit from the inventory the provisions, particularly corn, that would supply them for a year. Archaeological excavations and travelers' accounts are necessary additional sources. A more important deficiency is that land and its improvements were not listed and valued. Land and housing could not be concealed from heirs or legatees, and creditors could not seize land in payment. Hence the omission, but very inconvenient for the historian.

"Of course, because inventories supply mountains of data, very little use was made of them to create social landscapes until the advent of the computer. Computers can make quick and accurate counts of the hundreds or thousands of bits of information that large numbers of inventories provide. There is no longer the danger of generalizing from a few individuals whose typicality is undemonstrable. The computer has made possible the kind of social history that over the last twenty years has enriched our understanding of local place and enabled us to compare one place with another. Computers are not essential, however, if you are studying a small locality or selecting time by the slice rather than devouring it whole. What *is* essential for this kind of history is that you be willing to count."

Other records of economic life constitute a major resource for scholars of the past. According to Lorena Walsh, "plantation account books are a rich and so far little-mined source, and they survive in some numbers from the 1720s on. Now it is true that almost no yeoman farmers kept account books. Many could not read, write, or do arithmetic; others hadn't the leisure; and if some did keep accounts, they did not record them in durable bound ledgers that survived to end up in an archive. Nonetheless account books kept by big planters are often critical for understanding how tenants and yeoman landowners interacted with their neighbors. Exchanges between landlord and tenant are particularly revealing, showing for example the extent to which tenants often paid part of their rent in kind—chickens, eggs, and butter; spinning, weaving, sewing, and knitting; shoemaking, carpentry, harvest labor, and midwifery—as well as in cash crops or money. Maryland planters fairly consistently noted wives' and daughters' contributions to the family economy. Because big planters often paid out money that small planters owed to other people, one can sometimes glimpse the complexity and dense interconnections of the local economy, as well as understand just what yeoman men and women wanted to get for their labor.

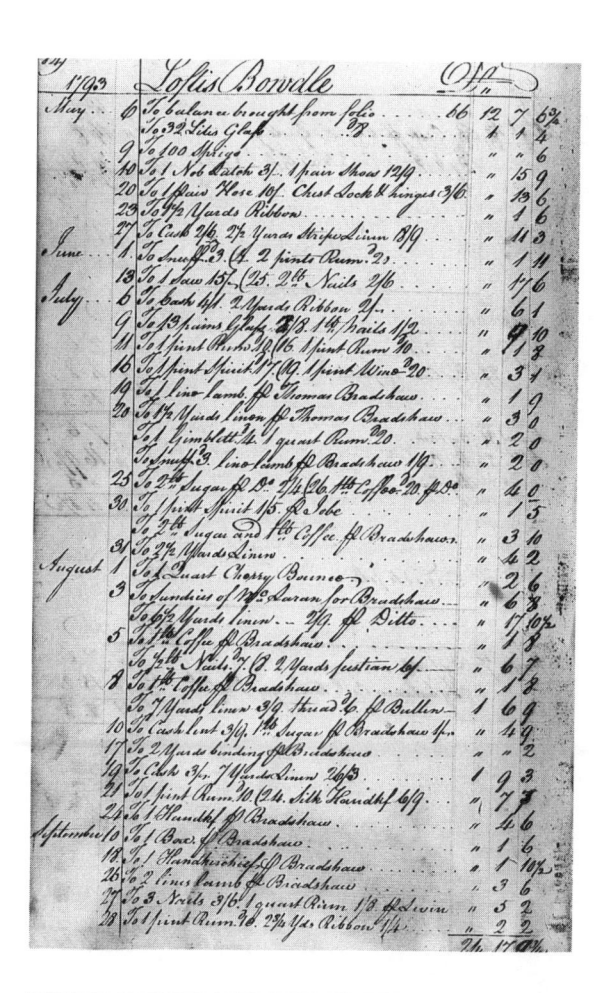

*Store accounts, such as this one, and planters' record books offer glimpses into the households of tenants and small planters. We can observe their purchases of clothing, tools, food, and drink and note their payments in cash or barter of produce, household crafts, and services.*

**Clues to the Past**     67

*The Cecil County assessor in 1783 listed the tracts held by county landowners. He also recorded the presence of houses, outbuildings, barns, orchards, mills, wharves, and warehouses; noted the quality of the land's location and soil; and itemized the acreage in arable, woods, and meadow.*

"Account books are not very easy sources to use. They are all kept in double entry form, but individuals made very different decisions about how they would handle various types of entries, cast balances, etc. It is often difficult to figure out what the debits and credits really represent—were they actual transfers of goods and services or mere accounting maneuvers? It helps if you already have some understanding of the economy of the area from which the account book comes. And you can better understand what is going on in one account book after you have studied several. Nonetheless, with time and patience much of the dynamics of local exchange and of networks of credit and debt can be teased out of them."

Individuals kept account books to track their own financial affairs, but governments also kept financial records as part of their administrative processes. Lois Carr observes that "in 1782, the new Maryland government began to tax property and the resulting tax assessments are a mine of information. The assessment of 1783, which survives for many Maryland counties, tells us who had land, its value and amount; the number, age category, and value of slaves; the value of plate and other personal property (household provisions, working tools, cash, and clothing were exempted); and the value of the whole taxable estate. For the years 1782 and 1783, paupers were listed, even though they paid no tax. Each household head was required to list the number of whites in his household, making it possible to enumerate the white population as well as virtually all of the black population (free black dependents appear to be missing). Finally, assessors included lists of the land tracts in the county, who owned them, the acreage in arable, woodland, and meadow, the characteristics of soil and location that affected value, the number and type of improvements, and the total value. From these lists you can gain details of the physical landscape at this particular time. The great value of the tax lists is that they provide information on types and total value of wealth for the living population."

Governments kept track of people as well as of taxable property. "The first census," notes Lois Carr, "was created in 1790 in order to establish the number of representatives for each state in the Congress. For each county, it named the head of each household and

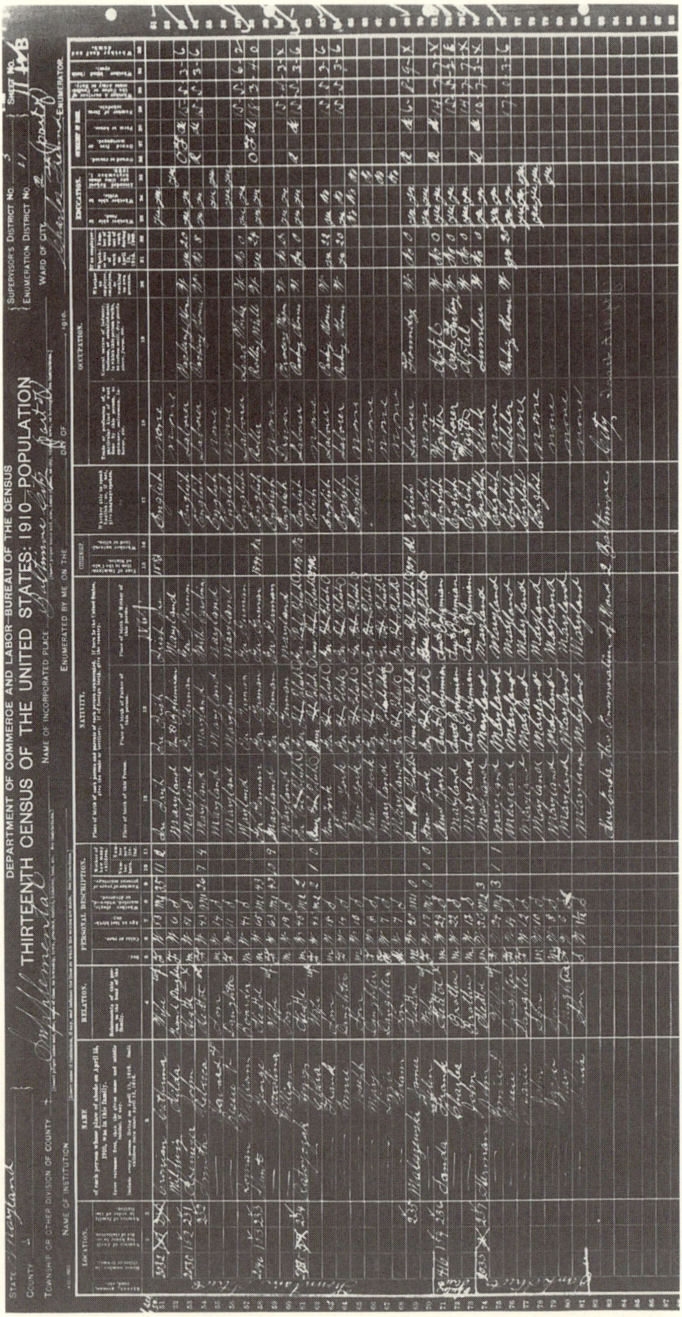
DEPARTMENT OF COMMERCE AND LABOR—BUREAU OF THE CENSUS

THIRTEENTH CENSUS OF THE UNITED STATES: 1910—POPULATION

showed the number of people in each by sex, age group, and race. Since 1790, the census has been taken every ten years, soon beginning to include more information on the growth of population and breakdowns by age and race. In 1820, the census taker began asking each person whether he was engaged in agriculture, commerce, or manufacturing, and noting who was an unnaturalized foreigner. In 1840, special schedules appear for the products of industry and agriculture and for schools. In 1850, the census began to list each family member, with exact age and place of birth, occupation, value of real estate owned, schooling, and ability to read and write. A variety of other schedules recorded mortality, births, marriages, and other social statistics.

"This accumulation of data can answer a variety of questions. Responses to place of birth supply information on migration patterns. District by district you can see the connection between area resources and occupations. The agricultural schedule allows one to determine the size and value of farms, amount and value of various crops, and the value of equipment used to produce them. From the schedule of products of industry, you can locate handcraft establishments, mills, factories, forges, and furnaces by area. In combination with the Martenet map, you can probably locate most of them exactly. The mortality schedules give an idea of

---

*The 1910 census takers recorded detailed information about the family background and employment of the residents in this working-class Baltimore neighborhood. The offspring of German and Polish immigrants, these men and women worked in packing houses and factories along the city's waterfront.*

the ages at which people died, reveal occupational hazards, and indicate the kinds of diseases that were prevalent."

For Linda Shopes, "the census of population—though obviously including people from all social strata—provides rich social data about working-class families, households, and communities. Beginning in 1850, individuals are listed, and working up to 1910 [the 1920 census will be available in 1992] the information gets increasingly more detailed. Thus by 1910 we can find out where a person lived, his or her name, relation to household head, sex, race, age, marital status, years in present marriage, number of children born and number alive, place of birth and parents' place of birth, whether or not one is a citizen, one's everyday language, occupation, and number of weeks unemployed in the past year, and information about literacy, home ownership, and physical disability. Furthermore, these enumerations are organized geographically by political jurisdiction—towns or wards within cities and, by 1880, relatively small enumeration districts within wards, whose boundaries are clearly noted. Beginning in 1880, street and house numbers are noted, and we can literally walk up and down the streets with the census taker, as he notes who lives at each address.

"You can perhaps imagine how this data can be used to delineate certain features of working-class life. In my own work, for example, I was able to identify hundreds of women cannery workers in the Fells Point district of Baltimore and come up with a composite description of them—age, ethnicity, marital status, etc. More than that, I was able to come up with some ideas about their family economy—noting, for example, that many of them had husbands who were seasonal workers along the docks, and that many of their children worked with them in the canneries rather than attend school. I was also able to identify a group of black oyster shuckers for a slightly earlier period, and found that they were more likely to have extended relatives and boarders living with them than were their white neighbors. Of course, the census itself doesn't explain why cannery women's children worked instead of attending school or why black shuckers had complex households. There are problems of interpretation that no single source will answer; addressing them is the intellectual challenge for the historian.

"The census of population is also not without its biases: people, especially from the lower socioeconomic groups, are sometimes omitted—perhaps the census taker hurried through their neighborhoods, perhaps they refused to answer his questions, perhaps they simply had no fixed address. Tracing people through twenty years of the census I have also found some disparities—ages are frequently not consistent and occasionally people list themselves as foreign born in one year, native born in another. The information was, after all, self-reported."

All of the scholars who participated in the conference or contributed additional material to this volume have worked with most of the sources described above. Some resources may have provided only a single clue, others may have contributed substantially to solving the historical puzzle. Rarely, however, does one source alone prove to be sufficient. The student of the past must be alert to the variety of sources, to the omissions as well as the inclusions, and to the imaginative ways in which seemingly mundane documents and objects can be made to help unlock the secrets of time.

# Interpreting the Past

Once the secrets of time have been uncovered, scholars still confront questions about how best to share with the general public the evidence they've gathered and the conclusions they've reached.

Many outdoor and historic site museums often use living history and first-person interpretation as tools to communicate with their audience. Historic St. Mary's City, for example, uses both techniques. First-person interpreters at the Godiah Spray tobacco plantation work the fields, tend the gardens, process crops, cook the meals—and talk to visitors who stop by to see their home. In other parts of the complex, actors following a prepared script re-enact historical events that have been carefully researched and reconstructed from court records and other documents.

Burton Kummerow, Director of Historic St. Mary's City, has called the seventeenth century, when St. Mary's was the capital of Maryland, "the ancient history of these United States." He goes on to observe that "the obscure and distant generations of immigrants who created the Chesapeake Tobacco Coast are hardly a single conscious thread in the fabric of the American psyche. When I left the ivory tower and was branded a 'generalist' by my specialist colleagues, I became fascinated by the task of pulling the public beyond the myths and platitudes. After all, shouldn't understanding be an important goal of our collective memory? Those of us who labor in the world of weekend excursions know how difficult it is to put flesh and blood on our ancestors.

"Never would I have imagined the many challenges I would face in the last decade at St. Mary's City. If ever there were a *hidden* heritage—literally hidden—it is the lost city of St. Mary's. Our fast-paced, very material culture can hardly conceive America's first frontier. We have a beautiful pastoral landscape that bears no resemblance to the seventeenth-century townlands. There are no surviving seventeenth-century structures in St. Mary's County. We do have millions of bits and pieces of trash discarded by our ancestors out their windows and over their fences, but, after twenty years of painstaking research, still no solid concept of what seventeenth-century St. Mary's looked like. We are dealing quite literally with a lost civilization.

"What then, as a museum staff devoted to truth in packaging, do we do for the visiting public? The first question from every new visitor is 'Where is the city?' A logical question from someone who most likely has explored the hundreds of surviving buildings at Colonial Williamsburg. The question, as you can imagine, has many answers. One answer, from two of the best

*The Godiah Spray plantation at Historic St. Mary's City recreates the landscape of a seventeenth-century settlement. Interpreters in costume and in character bring that landscape to life.*

researchers in the business, historian Lois Carr and archaeologist Henry Miller, is—come along with us, get down in the dirt, read a quaint and curious old document, sign on to a modern voyage of discovery. The process of good research can be, in itself, good interpretation.

"My task is to explore another answer. The small fraternity of seventeenth-century museums, faced with a dearth of traditional museum tools, has stretched the frontiers of museum education. The excitement is in the human experience. What better story is there for Americans than the insurmountable odds of the Chesapeake frontier—disease and early death, back-breaking and monotonous work, terrible dislocation and loneliness—all conquered by the grit and determination of the indomitable human spirit. Like other 'lost' seventeenth-century sites, we've built high quality 'sets'—buildings, fences, gardens, furniture, livestock (all of which can be improved as we learn more), put on costumes, and dipped into the bag of tricks developed over the centuries by the acting community. What results is the so-called living history, the time machine that takes artifacts out of cases and puts museum visitors face to face with their past.

"Living history is certainly no panacea. We all know the past is dead and gone and we are locked right here in the present. It is a tool of the informed imagination, no better or worse than any other device. This tool is not for everyone, but when it works it is magic. The device is a mixture of entertainment and education that easily cuts through age, class, and level of education."

Another living history museum, the 1840 House, part of the complex that makes up the Baltimore City Life Museums, is dedicated to interpreting "the lives of ordinary people—working men and women, children, blacks and whites—who traditionally have had no one to tell their stories." Census records document the residents of the house in 1840: owner John Hutchinson, his wife and three daughters, an apprentice, a boarder, and a free black woman and a young girl. The census, moreover, provides ages and occupations, as well as race and sex, for the inhabitants and offers evidence of social and economic status. Hutchinson's inventory supplies the historical basis for furnishing the interior rooms of the house. Because curators have used reproductions for most of the furnishings, visitors can enter directly into the world of 1840 Baltimore; they "can lie on rope beds, sit on horsehair sofas, and cook on the open hearth in the kitchen."

Director of Interpretation Dale Jones describes the living history programs of the 1840 House in terms that echo the comments of Burt Kummerow. The goal, he notes, is to keep people entertained *and* to educate them. "The reality," for museum staff, "is that the museum is in competition with other forms of entertainment. At the same time, museums are different because they are also trying to educate their audiences. It is important both that the audience has fun in a museum and also learns a little." Museums that interpret their site through living history have an advantage over traditional museums in that they have a captive audience. Interpreters may have twenty to thirty minutes in which to communicate with their viewers rather than the few seconds that most museum visitors spend reading exhibit labels. But because the audience is captive, it is imperative, Jones notes, that they enjoy themselves while they are participating in an interpretive program.

Living history, Jones observes, offers a range of interpretive styles. Interpreters can simply be dressed in period clothing as part of the museum props, they can do demonstrations, they can represent a character, or they can play a character; programs can feature one-person or interactive scripted performances. Flexibility extends beyond the role of the interpreters, however, in ways that represent the strength of living history interpretations. "They can elucidate a time period or an issue that is difficult, at least from the audience standpoint, to interpret through traditional methods." Programs at

*Living history programs at the 1840 House address social issues that Baltimoreans faced in the 1830s and 1840s, including colonization and abolitionism. In this scene, Darius Stokes, a free black preacher, teacher, and drayman, debates with Sarah West, the Hutchinson's free black servant, about whether she should leave America and move to Liberia.*

the 1840 House, for example, focus on racial issues, including abolition, using the living history format "to create empathy on the part of the audience with the time period and the characters." Other programs examine the ideal of womanhood and domesticity that shaped women's lives in the mid-nineteenth century.

Starting with an emphasis on "historical plausibility, we try to set up situations that could have happened and make them come to life. Our goal is to stimulate the audience to look at issues from different sides." Primary material, culled from newspapers, city directories, and census records, is merged with secondary sources to study the impact of issues on the family's daily life. The process provides "a means of getting to the lives of ordinary people for whom we don't have much other evidence that can be effectively displayed," according to Jones.

While the specific site and the criterion of historical plausibility impose certain limitations on the range of issues and social groups that can be portrayed, the medium itself embodies a high degree of imaginative flexibility. Changing an exhibit, for example, can be accomplished not by the installation of new artifacts, but simply by changing the script given to the actors. Interpreters cannot plausibly present material that historically occurred after the 1840s, but scripts can allow them to incorporate events from the past. One 1840 House program, for example, focused on the War of 1812 by employing a sequence of daydreams by a central character to recreate past events. The Hutchinsons' servant, Margaret Malloy, returned to her home after a day in which she observed celebrations commemorating the war. Tired from her day's work, she sat down to rest in her living room and began dreaming about the war; one character in her dream, Mary Pickersgill, then took up the narrative of the scene. A second reverie in the next room brought to life three veterans reminiscing about their wartime experiences and a third dream sequence in yet another room featured Francis Scott Key. Thus by the plausible device of enacting the dreams of a historically valid character, the interpretation could be guided to specific events outside the direct experience of the residents of the house.

Many programs at the 1840 House are also designed to bring visitors directly into the interpretive experience. Groups can "spend an entire night living in the past," including preparing a meal over the open hearth, eating that meal by candlelight in the upstairs parlor, playing nineteenth-century parlor games such as shadow buff and tableaux vivants, and sleeping in the house. For those visitors who make a shorter visit to the house, demonstrations of cooking, needlework, music, and dance offer visitors direct experiences of processes of nineteenth-century work and play. The goal is to entertain visitors in ways that enhance their understanding of a historical time and place.

Decorative arts historians Jennifer Goldsborough and Gregory Weidman, both curators at the Maryland Historical Society, face a different challenge. Because the Society is "The Museum and Library of Maryland History," Goldsborough and Weidman employ artifacts of material culture as devices to explore historical themes and settings and must employ the same techniques of detective work that academic historians use to uncover the full stories of their artifacts. The recent exhibit, "Joshua Johnson: Freeman and Early American Portrait Painter," for example, encompassed study not only of Johnson's paintings, but also the works of contemporary artists and detailed histories of Johnson's subjects in order to illuminate Johnson's place as an artist and the world in which he worked.

Detailed examination of the physical remains of Johnson's work—the paintings themselves—revealed characteristics that could be used both to establish the authenticity of questionable works and also to assess Johnson's economic status. "More than any other artist of the period, Johnson used every fragment of his material." The wood pieces Johnson used for stretchers tended to be thinner than those of other artists; he covered his frames with a minimum of fabric, leaving little surplus beyond the row of tacks that held cloth to frame. Paintings believed to be the work of Johnson that exhibit these characteristics can thus be credited to his hand. At the same time, the frugal use of materials provides eloquent testimony to the lack of financial prosperity that Johnson derived from his painting.

Careful comparative analysis of Johnson's subjects with those of other contemporary Baltimore artists similarly reveals the circumscribed social and cultural world within which Johnson worked. Johnson, for example, painted a disproportionate number of children. According to Jennifer Goldsborough, a definite hierarchy of artist and sitter existed in nineteenth-century Maryland. It was common practice for a top-level artist to paint the portrait of the head of the family, for a second-tier artist to paint his wife's portrait, and for a third-rank artist to paint his children. During his early career, when Joshua Johnson painted members of prominent Baltimore families, he usually painted the children. At the same time, Johnson's adult subjects were his neighbors in the Old Town and Fells Point neighborhoods of Baltimore, members of the upwardly mobile middle and artisan classes who did not ordinarily have their portraits painted. Goldsborough and Weidman suspect that Johnson painted many of these portraits through a barter arrangement, exchanging the portrait for goods that these neighbors could supply.

Study of Johnson's subjects offers insights into both the black and white communities of early nineteenth-century Baltimore. For example, Johnson painted several of his female subjects holding a book. Curators Weidman and Goldsborough, knowing from census records, city directories, diaries, and letters that the women's occupations and lifestyles left little leisure time for reading, infer that these women nonetheless wanted their portraits to let viewers know that they were educated women who could read. Similarly, the curators

> **Portrait Painting.**
>
> THE subscriber, grateful for the liberal encouragement which an indulgent public have conferred on him, in his first essays, in PORTRAIT PAINTING, returns his sincere acknowledgments.
>
> He takes liberty to observe, That by dint of industrious application, he has so far improved and matured his talents, that he can insure the most precise and natural likenesses.
>
> As a *self-taught genius*, deriving from nature and industry his knowledge of the Art; and having experienced many insuperable obstacles in the pursuit of his studies, it is highly gratifying to him to make assurances of his ability to execute all commands, with an effect, and in a style, which must give satisfaction. He therefore respectfully solicits encouragement. ☞ Apply at his House, in the Alley leading from *Charles* to *Hanover Street*, back of *Sears*'s Tavern.
>
> **JOSHUA JOHNSTON.**

*Joshua Johnson's advertisement of his services as a portrait painter, describing his abilities and his training, also gave his address so that potential customers could call and arrange for a portrait. Curators used that information as part of their reconstruction of the network of Johnson's subjects.*

*Interpreting the Past*

*This portrait of Mrs. Thomas Everette and her children is the only Johnson portrait documented to him in family papers. Mrs. Everette willed her eldest daughter "the large family painting of my self and 5 children painted by J Johnson in 1818. . . ." In this portrait, with Mrs. Everette holding her youngest child, two of the sons hold books.*

knew that Johnson's portraits included four paintings of black men. Using city directories and census, newspaper, and probate records, Weidman traced the families of those four men to determine the history of the paintings, a process that revealed the gradual disintegration over time of the free black community in antebellum Baltimore. The families, who were fairly prosperous at the beginning of the nineteenth century, gradually declined in status and after mid-century were much more difficult to trace in the city records. Johnson's portraits thus "provide windows into categories of people for whom we don't have good documentary evidence, including blacks, women, and lower-middle-class communities."

One basic piece of detective work involved verifying that Joshua Johnson was indeed a free black. Researchers had been looking since the 1920s for conclusive proof of Johnson's status but without success. "We hoped that Johnson would retain his position as the earliest known black American artist for whom a body of extant works survive, not just because he was a talented artist but because he had attained his profession by overcoming 'insuperable' odds that beleaguered him and others of his race and time. Johnson traditionally has served as the stepping stone into the subject of black art and artists in America. Yet we were prepared to rewrite this history if the documentation we found confirmed that Johnson was white or of some race other than black." The uncertainty was resolved when Weidman, unable to find a "Joshua Johnson" in the 1810 census index, a year in which Johnson's place of residence was known from the city directory, realized that the entry for "Josa Johnston" might well be the missing proof. The original census document indeed revealed that the entry was written as "Jo$^{sa}$," the period abbreviation for "Joshua," and had been misinterpreted by the indexer. Weidman's search demonstrated both the value of persistence in research and the need to interpret the use made by secondary sources of original materials. In this case, the census document described the household of Johnson in 1810 as consisting only of six free blacks, the proof needed to confirm Joshua Johnson's status as a free black artist.

A third type of history museum, the industrial muse-

*Interpreting the Past*   85

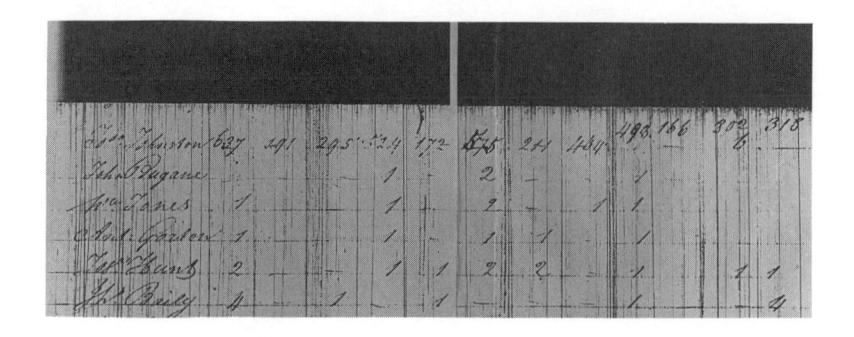

*The entry for Jo^sa Johnston in the 1810 census, with six free blacks in the household, confirms Johnson's status as a free black artist.*

um, also provides avenues of access into the lives of communities that traditional history has often neglected. The modern industrial museum is, as the adjective connotes, a development of the last few decades. Previously, industrial history, according to Baltimore Museum of Industry director Dennis Zembala, reached the public through one of three earlier museum types: either the large museum of science and industry that displayed industrial artifacts, or the site-specific museums located in grist or textile mills or iron furnaces, or company museums that focused on the history of a particular firm. In all three types of museum, the emphasis of exhibits and interpretation concentrated upon the product and perhaps the technical processes of production; broader questions of work environments and work forces received little if any attention.

The growth of interest during the last few decades on the part of academic historians in social history necessarily directed attention toward broader questions of

*Children role-playing as nineteenth-century oyster shuckers at The Cannery, an interactive workplace activity center at the Baltimore Museum of Industry.*

industrial history. Dennis Zembala, in "Now, Industrial History Moves Front and Center" (*Museum News* [November/December 1990]: 34–37), says "Because most people spend so much time working, it was only logical that industrial history should emerge as an important part of this new focus [on history as a] mirror of life.... Knowledge of work processes and technology helps evaluate the nature of skill, the impact of industrialization on craftsmen, patterns of urban growth, occupational mobility, and a host of other concerns."

The Baltimore Museum of Industry was founded in 1978 with the goal of "interpreting and presenting the impact of industrialization on a community and its people." The museum sought to examine the interaction of changing industrial technology with local, urban, social, and labor history, beginning with the core exhibit, "The Way We Worked: Baltimore's People, Port, and Industry." The aim was to "encourage visitors to examine their own attitudes toward work and their working heritage."

Curators and exhibit designers have employed a multitude of interpretive methods to achieve that goal. Some exhibits feature re-created work settings; others offer visitors the opportunity to engage in hands-on activities. Interpreters may offer demonstrations of machinery or they may provide guided tours of exhibit areas. Oral histories vividly convey the daily routines of the men and women who comprised the labor force in mills and factories. The growth and decline of Baltimore's industrial sector shaped the city's demographic structure, culture, class relations, racial makeup, neighborhood development, and numerous other aspects of its history over the last century. The industrial museum seeks to inform its visitors about those relationships by offering them the opportunity to observe and participate in a process that affected thousands of ordinary people.

# The Future of the Past: An Evaluation

## GEORGE H. CALLCOTT

*Unlocking the Secrets of Time* is dedicated not only to understanding the past, but to the still larger questions of how we understand history and what we make of it. These larger questions preoccupied historians back in the days of Kant and Hegel, of Croce and Collingwood, of Carl Becker and Charles A. Beard. Then, during the 1960s and 1970s we largely set aside the philosophical questions. Although research surged ahead, the enrollments in our classes declined, and the public began to look the other way. Now, at the end of the 1980s, we are beginning to ask the big questions, conferences like that held in Annapolis in 1989 are requiring us to consider what we are really doing, and the public interest in history is surging.

The program for the November 1989 conference demonstrates the vigor and direction of our pursuit of the past. It dwelled on new techniques for understanding: record stripping, information retrieval, and quantification; oral history and use of illustrations; archaeology, material culture, and the popularization of the past through restorations and even dramatic recreations; the use of concepts from anthropology, sociology, psychology, literary criticism, and the hard sciences. Consider this as a generalization: most historians are making their contribution today at the point at which history intersects with other disciplines.

Along with new techniques, our interests are turning toward new fields of history. Not one of the conference sessions dealt mainly with politics, or wars, or even with history-as-events of any sort. Instead, we have grown fascinated with the various manifestations of social history: how people in the past really lived and thought; the role of elites and of ordinary people, of small farmers, blacks, women, and families; the mentality of different periods; how groups form and operate; the meaning of community.

The other main new field of history nowadays is local history. Even a decade ago, conferences dedicated specifically to Maryland were almost unknown. Now, thanks largely to the Maryland Humanities Council, they are occurring two and three times a year, with a high degree of public involvement in these activities. Local studies, which used to be considered quaint and antiquarian, are now winning top prizes at the conventions of professional historians. The grand theories that excited us a few years ago have grown pale, and it is the particularities, concrete and real, that seem to provide us nowadays with the largest understanding of the past.

The November conference did not concern itself much with a philosophy to contain our expanding activities—a rationale for our new directions. The absence

*A variety of sources provide clues to the amusements of the past. This 1928 cover of* Life *magazine, itself a part of popular culture, captures the dance craze of the 1920s.*

of rationale, however, may be a sign of confidence. Mostly, historians seem to be saying, quite simply, that history for society is much like memory for an individual. It provides us with identity and direction. Insofar as we find meaning in the conglomerate of our past experience—either as individuals or as society—then we find confidence in ourselves and coherence as a society. Insofar as we fail to come to terms with the conglomerate of our past experience, then our lives and our society are only one thing after another, existential and meaningless.

Several of the conference speakers called attention to the dual role of historians, first as gatherers of data and then as commentators upon it. This distinction is important. We used to think that data gathering and commentary were the same, that data *was* history, that the facts spoke for themselves. We used to speak of historians filling in pieces of a puzzle that eventually would reveal an ultimate truth. That image has given way in recent years to a realization that the data of the past, like the data on which our memory draws, is nearly infinite and nearly worthless without our ordering of it. Beyond our role of data gatherers, we are commentators on history—commentators in constant dialogue with the past, constantly drawing up new data and rearranging it to meet changing needs. We as individuals draw up different data from memory depending on our immediate concerns, and we as historians draw up different data from history for our society.

The historian-commentator, then, becomes as important as the data from which he or she is drawing. The historian-commentator is a high priest of society, utilizing its data bank to define society's present experience and utilizing the present experience to find meaning in the past. Each one of us as audience sifts the commentary again, ignoring or finding credibility in what we hear and read about history. We judge the historian useful in proportion to his or her persuasiveness and relevance.

This leaves us with a certain relativism, such as R. G. Collingwood and Carl Becker discovered long ago, but our changing interpretations are not idiosyncratic or circular. The meaning we find today in America's settlement, in George Washington, or in the Civil War is not only different from what it used to be but far deeper. Each commentator adds to the conversation about the past, the conversation evolves, and understanding expands. We are not much listened to unless we can add something new and relevant. Each commentator stands on the shoulders of all who went before, even as in the sciences, utilizing the data and insights of predecessors, and drawing on new data and insights in the light of new experience.

Let us come back, then, to the theme of this volume: how will we study history and make use of it in the future? Now, at least, the study of the past is flourishing—with new data, new techniques, new fields of investigation, and new conclusions. Perhaps never before have our questions been so large and exciting, our confidence in what we do secure, and our promise so great. The future of the past is rich, and we are having fun with what we do. When the future of history is bright, that might even be a sign that the health and future of our society is bright as well.

# *Exploring the Past*
## JEAN B. RUSSO

The Stage Manager and observer of life in Grover's Corners noted in Act I of *Our Town* that "Babylon once had two million people in it, and all we know about 'm is the names of the kings and some copies of wheat contracts and—the sales of slaves.... And even in Greece and Rome, all we know about the real life of the people is what we can piece together out of the joking poems and the comedies they wrote for the theatre back then." His remarks reflect one concern of *Unlocking the Secrets of Time:* how we can learn about past societies and peoples, how we can piece together, out of often meager clues, the nature of their lives.

He went on to say, "I'm having a copy of this play put in a cornerstone so the people a thousand years from now'll know a few simple facts about us—more than the Treaty of Versailles and the Lindbergh flight.... this is the way we were in the provinces North of New York at the beginning of the Twentieth Century, ... in our growing up and in our marrying, and in our living, and in our dying." A second concern: what do we save for the future to help them understand the present?

Historians must weigh and sift bits and pieces of evidence, try to clarify ambiguities, deal with lacunae in the sources, and attempt to resolve apparent contradictions in the historical record. Their writings usually represent the results of that process of evaluation and judgment, rather than revealing the process itself. A few scholars, however, share the process with their readers. In one noted recent work in this vein, *The Kindness of Strangers: The Abandonment of Children in Western Europe from Late Antiquity to the Renaissance* (Pantheon, 1988), historian John Boswell explores a subject upon which the historical record remains virtually silent. The result, as David Gate noted in *Newsweek,* is a book whose "ultimate value may be to show how a good historian works when there's next to nothing to work with.... Even general readers may be less interested in lost children of long ago than in the process of research and reasoning by which Boswell tries to rescue them from the great stillness." Similarly, Carlo Ginzburg, "a historian with an insatiable curiosity who pursues even the faintest of clues with all the zest of a born detective" (J. H. Elliott, in the *New York Review of Books*), explores the questions of historical method and historical knowledge in *Clues, Myths, and the Historical Method* (Johns Hopkins University Press, 1988). Ginzburg draws upon anthropology, art history, comparative religion and myth, and psychoanalytic literature to retrieve the cultural and social past that, as the Stage Manager noted, conventional historical sources ignore.

In the hands of qualified practitioners, oral history

provides a fruitful methodology for recovering the history of everyday life in the twentieth century. The fall 1989 issue of *Maryland Humanities* contains one example, in the form of an essay by State Comptroller Louis Goldstein, reminiscing about events and changes that he has observed during his lifetime. Willa Baum's *Oral History for the Local Historical Society* (American Association for State and Local History [AASLH], 1988) serves as the basic text for organizing and managing a local oral history program. Linda Shopes's article, "Beyond Trivia and Nostalgia: Collaborating in the Construction of a Local History" (*International Journal of Oral History*, vol. 5, 1984), provides a critique of the pitfalls that can accompany such projects, while the interpretive issues involved in using oral sources are explored by Paul Thompson in *The Voice of the Past: Oral History* (Oxford University Press, 1988).

Photographs offer a second window into the recent past, with a view that extends back to mid-nineteenth century. One of the most notable collections of historic Maryland photographs can be found in Mame Warren and Marion E. Warren's *Maryland Time Exposures, 1840–1940* (Johns Hopkins University Press, 1984), whose production was supported by a grant from the Maryland Humanities Council. The Baltimore Heritage Neighborhood Project—again supported by the Council—combined photographs and oral history to produce *Baltimore People, Baltimore Places: A Neighborhood Album* as both a traveling exhibition and a publication. Photographs also form a major portion of a valuable resource, The History of Maryland Slide Collection (Constance B. Schulz, editor; 1980).

Sources for local history receive attention also from

*Colonies and then states printed their own money until the nineteenth century. This bill was issued by the state of Maryland in 1780. Eventually the federal government would assume control of the currency; money would no longer be issued by individual banks or by states. This piece of currency thus documents one aspect of the gradual shift of power from individual states to the federal government.*

Charles Faulkner Bryan, Jr., and Mark V. Wetherington in *Finding Our Past: A Guidebook for Group Projects in Community History* (East Tennessee Historical Society, 1983), the product of an NEH-funded project on local history. Local history also provides the focus for the activities of the American Association for State and Local History. The Society's catalog of publications lists a wide range of material dealing with all aspects of local history. Members of the organization also receive a bimonthly magazine, *History News,* whose articles routinely explore topics related to the themes of this conference. The AASLH also provides research grants and conference funding for projects promoting the study of local history. A recent conference featured David Kyvig and Myron Marty, authors of a pioneering book on the study of local history, *Nearby History: Exploring the Past around You.*

Historical interpretations are not absolutes, remaining fixed and immutable over time. Rather, as the existence of courses and books on historiography tells us, they reflect the times—the concerns, the biases, the issues—in which they were written. Numerous works by philosophers and historians have explored the study of history as a discipline, both as practitioners seeking to define the nature of their craft and as critics examining the interaction between the historian and the culture of his times. Classic and influential examples of these themes include R. G. Collingwood's *The Idea of History* (1946) and Herbert Butterfield's *The Whig Interpretation of History* (1931); David Hackett Fischer provides a trenchant survey of the practice of history in *Historical Fallacies* (Harper and Row, 1970). Other works consider these questions from special vantage points. John Higham's *History: Professional Scholarship in America* (Johns Hopkins University Press, 1983), for example, traces the development of the profession in the United States, analyzing the evolution of new interpretive schools in reaction to the views of their predecessors.

Thematic works address the same questions from a slightly different perspective. The recent celebration of the bicentennials of the Revolution and Constitution, for example, have prompted historians to explore the use that we as a nation have made of our past, and particularly of its mythic symbols. Karal Ann Marling examines the iconic meaning of George Washington in *George Washington Slept Here: Colonial Revivals and American Culture, 1876-1986* (Harvard University Press, 1988); Wilbur Zelinsky considers the same theme more broadly in *Nation into State: The Shifting Symbolic Foundations of American Nationalism* (University of North Carolina Press, 1988). One of the most profound and far-ranging explorations of the interaction between past and present—of how the past is known and how it is reshaped to suit the needs of the present—appears in David Lowenthal's *The Past Is a Foreign Country* (Cambridge University Press, 1985).

Those interested specifically in exploring ways to unlock Maryland's hidden heritage are particularly fortunate. Some of the most insightful scholarship drawing upon new sources can be found in the field of colonial Chesapeake history, stimulated by the innovative work of Lois Green Carr as historian for the St. Mary's City Commission and of those who have collaborated with or been inspired by her. The fruits of their efforts can be sampled in *Law, Society, and Politics in Early Maryland* (Johns Hopkins University Press, 1977), *The Chesapeake in the Seventeenth Century: Essays on Anglo-American Society and Politics* (University of North Carolina Press, 1979) and *Colonial Chesapeake Society* (University of North Carolina Presss, 1988). Robert J. Brugger's masterful survey of Maryland history, *Maryland: A Middle Temperament, 1634-1980* (Johns Hopkins University Press, 1988), weaves together the work of these and many other scholars, profiting from his

*Exploring the Past* 99

*Family portraits preserve the likenesses of members for future generations, documenting family genealogy (five generations, each identified, appear in this photograph). Used collectively, these photographs tell us of styles of dress, family demographics, standards of living, work lives, and other aspects of family and cultural history.*

and their utilization of virtually all the sources available for the exploration of Maryland's past. George H. Callcott's *Maryland and America, 1940 to 1980* (Johns Hopkins University Press, 1985) merits attention for its exemplary use and discussion of contemporary sources.

Our present will be the future's past. What are we leaving in the way of clues and how will the future deal with that evidence? Scholars of ancient and medieval history have to tease information out of elusive bits of evidence. Future scholars may instead have to grapple with too much information, while contemporary curators, archivists, and other repository administrators must sift and winnow to avoid being overwhelmed by information and artifacts. Curators must determine what to save of today for the use of tomorrow. But while collections policies represent one aspect of saving the present, changing technology presents another and equally knotty challenge.

Many of the records of modern society—census data, tax assessments, voting lists, to name only a few—that historians rely upon for a myriad of uses are now being retained not on paper but on computer disk and tape. Computer technology, however, changes much more rapidly than print technology. The disintegration of books and other documents printed since the nineteenth century on acidic paper presents archivists, curators, and librarians with a formidable preservation task, but the rapid obsolescence of computer hardware and software may pose an even greater challenge. Will we have to keep a working inventory of outmoded computers and antique software to be able to retrieve data currently being stored on disk and tape? Professional journals and newsletters, like *The Chronicle of Higher Education,* the American Historical Association's *Perspectives,* and the *Newsletter* of the Organization of American Historians, are beginning to address these issues.

Museum curators and other exhibit designers continually confront the question of how to present history to the public. No exhibit can fully comprehend any aspect of the past; choices must be made—about themes, about evidence, about interpretation. Alfred Young, a distinguished historian who served as curator for an exhibit at the Chicago Historical Society on the Bicentennial of the Constitution, reflected upon the dilemma in an article entitled "The Historian as Museum Curator," reprinted in the October 1988 issue of *Perspectives*. Contributors to *Past Meets Present: Essays about Historic Interpretation and Public Audiences* (Jo Blatti, editor; 1987) similarly examine—as academic historians or museum professionals—the issue of balancing aesthetic, pedagogic, and scholarly elements in the development of museum exhibits and programs. Recent exhibits at the Smithsonian's National Museum of American History—"A Material World," "Field to Factory," "A More Perfect Union," "After the Revolution: Everyday Life in America," and "Men and Women: Costume, Gender, and Power"—challenge viewers to look at familiar objects or familiar history in new ways and use a wide variety of ordinary as well as unusual artifacts to issue that challenge.

For those interested in further exploration of these themes, newsletters and journals provide a continuing forum for discussion. Mention has already been made of AASLH's *History News*. Other sources include articles in or special issues of *Preservation News*, published by the National Trust for Historic Preservation; *The American Historical Review*, the journal of the American Historical Association; *The Journal of American History*, published by the Organization of American Historians; and *The Chronicle of Higher Education*.

Scholars do not have a monopoly on historical research, however; the major area collections are open to the public, professional and amateur alike. The Maryland State Archives serves as repository for state and county public records as well as for other manuscript source material; the Maryland Historical Society has some public records and an extensive manuscripts collection and library of genealogical material; and county historical societies have libraries and collections of artifacts. The National Archives, Smithsonian Institutions (particularly the Museum of American History), and the Library of Congress offer unparalleled resources for the exploration of almost any historical topic. The staffs of these various organizations can provide valuable assistance in locating material in their own collections and in suggesting other repositories that might be helpful. The keys to unlocking Maryland's hidden heritage await anyone who wishes to use them.

ILLUSTRATION CREDITS

The figure on page vi is from John Smith, Virginia, 1608 (1612), MSA SC 1213-257, Maryland State Archives. The figures on pages x, 10, 26, 84, 86, and 97 are from Maryland Historical Society. The figure at top of page 6 is a detail from Plate 1, in *An Account of the Municipal Celebration of the One Hundred and Fiftieth Anniversary of the Settlement of Baltimore*, ed. Edward Spencer (Baltimore: King Brothers, 1881). The figure on page 6 lower left is from *Maryland Line Confederate Soldier's Home*, Pikesville, Maryland, comp. by Capt. George W. Booth (Board of Governors and Managers, 1894). The figure on page 6 lower right is from MSA SC G2106, Maryland State Archives. The figure on page 15 is from MSA SC 1427-6, Maryland State Archives. The figure on page 16 is from MS220, Box 6, Letter from Charles Carroll to sons Charles and Daniel, July 7, 1719, Carroll-McTavish Papers, Maryland Historical Society. The photograph on page 16 is by Simon Marsden. The top figure on page 21 is from the Gilman School Archives. The two photographs at bottom of page 21 are by David Enders Tripp. The figure on page 27 is *The Dinner Party*, by Henry Sargent, gift of Mrs. Horatio Lamb in memory of Mr. and Mrs. Winthrop Sargent, courtesy, Museum of Fine Arts, Boston. The figure on page 28 is from Baltimore County, Register of Wills (Inventories) 42, f.89, MSA C340, Maryland State Archives. The figures on pages 33, 36, 37, and 76 are from Historic St. Mary's City. The drawing on page 41 is by Nancy Kurtz, Maryland Historical Trust. The photograph on page 42 is by John Vachon, U.S. Dept. of Agriculture, Farm Security Administration, negative no. 1384-M2, Library of Congress. The photographs on page 43 are from Special Collections, Albin O. Kuhn Library, University of Maryland–Baltimore County. The figures on pages 47, 49, and 91 are from the Library of Congress. The figure on page 54 is from MSA SC 1427-286, Maryland State Archives. The figure on page 56 is from MSA SC 2140-480, Maryland State Archives. The figure on page 59 is from MS220, Box 1, Inventory of Charles Carroll's apparel, Ledger X, Carroll-McTavish Papers. The figure on page 61 is from Prerogative Court (Accounts) 66, f.63, MSA S531, Maryland State Archives. The figure on page 63 is from Prerogative Court (Inventories) 1, f.92, MSA S534, Maryland State Archives. The figure on page 67 is from Jesse Richardson, Ledger C, 1793–1794, Chancery Papers (Exhibits), MSA SC 1878-0034, Maryland State Archives. The figure on page 68 is from General Assembly House of Delegates (Assessment Record), Cecil County, 5th District Real Property, f.1, MSA 1161-4-4-1CE, Maryland State Archives. The figure on page 70 is from U.S. Census Bureau (Census Record) MD, 1910, f.11b, Baltimore City, MSA M3255, Maryland State Archives. The figure on page 79 is from Baltimore City Life Museums. The figure on page 83 is from *Baltimore Intelligencer*, December 19, 1793. The figure on page 87 is from Edwin H. Remsberg / Baltimore Museum of Industry, copyright 1991. The photograph on page 100 is from MSA SC 1477-6814, Maryland State Archives.

# Conference Participants

Dr. Elizabeth Baer, Provost and Dean of the College, Washington College, Moderator, "Notable Marylanders: Ordinary People," Workshop C

Dr. Carl Bode, Professor of English Emeritus, University of Maryland–College Park, "Acres of Diamonds"

Dr. Elaine G. Breslaw, Professor of History, Morgan State College, Commentary, "The Music of the Tuesday Club"

Dr. Robert J. Brugger, Editor, The Johns Hopkins University Press, "How Recent Discoveries Have Changed Our View of Maryland's Past," Plenary Session

Dr. George H. Callcott, Professor of History, University of Maryland–College Park, "The Future of the Past: An Evaluation"

Dr. Lois Green Carr, Historian, Historic St. Mary's City, "The Head of the Bay," Workshop A

Dr. Naomi Collins, Executive Director, Maryland Humanities Council

Honorable Gilbert Gude, Director, Potomac River Basin Consortium, "Along the Potomac," Workshop A

Dr. Ronald Hoffman, Professor of History, University of Maryland–College Park, "The Written Record: Expected and Unexpected Sources," Workshop B

Dr. Freeman Hrabowski, III, Vice-Provost, University of Maryland–Baltimore County, Moderator, "The Carroll Family: Shapers of Maryland and the Nation," Workshop B

Mr. Paul Hundley, State Underwater Archaeologist, Maryland Historical Trust, "Maryland Waters Remember," Plenary Session

Mr. Barry Kessler, Assistant Director and Curator, Jewish Historical Society, "Representing the Carrolls: The Challenge of Interpreting the Carroll Mansion," Workshop B

Mr. Burton K. Kummerow, Executive Director, Historic St. Mary's City, Commentary, "Voices from the Past: The Trial of Josias Fendall"

Dr. Peter Lade, Professor of Anthropology, Salisbury State University, "Using Technology to Reveal the Past," Plenary Session

Dr. Mark Leone, Professor of Anthropology, University of Maryland–College Park, Moderator, "Our Towns: A Sense of Place," Workshop A

Dr. Charles McGovern, Curator, Division of Community Life, National Museum of American History, Smithsonian Institution, "Saving Today for Tomorrow," Plenary Session

Dr. Henry Miller, Director of Research, Historic St. Mary's City, "Revealing Maryland's First Capital: Archaeology at St. Mary's City," Workshop A

Mr. Steven C. Newsome, Director, Anacostia Museum, Smithsonian Institution, "Reconstructing an Urban Black Community," Workshop C

Dr. Edward C. Papenfuse, State Archivist, Maryland State Archives, Moderator, "The Future of the Past," Plenary Session

Dr. Jean B. Russo, Director of Research, Historic Annapolis Foundation, Conference Director

Dr. Linda Shopes, Associate Historian, Pennsylvania Historical and Museum Commission, "Uncovering Working-Class History," Workshop C

Dr. Gregory A. Stiverson, Assistant State Archivist, Maryland State Archives, "Ugly Babies and Tiny Toes: Reflections on the Art of History"

Ms. Susan G. Tripp, Director, University Collections, The Johns Hopkins University, "Homewood: The Country Seat of Charles Carroll, Jr.," Workshop B

Dr. Lorena S. Walsh, Research Fellow, The Colonial Williamsburg Foundation, "The Yeoman Family Farmer," Workshop C

# Index

Account book, 66-69
Accounts. *See* Probate records
African Americans, 29, 57-58; in antebellum Baltimore, 84-85; history of, 45; institutions of, 53-57; sources, 45-46; in urban areas, 44-46
*Afro-American*, 46
American Association for State and Local History, 96, 97, 102
American Historical Association, 101, 102
Annapolis, 13, 17, 58
Anne Arundel County, 42
Archaeology, 19, 31-32; sites, 39; underwater (marine), 38, 39-40
Artifacts, 19, 25, 31, 32, 33, 81
Assessments, 69, 101

Baer, Elizabeth, 104
Baker, John, 34
Baltimore, 13, 46, 82, 83
Baltimore City Life Museums, 23, 77
Baltimore Heritage Neighborhood Project, 96
Baltimore Museum of Industry, 86, 87-88
Barney Flotilla, 39
Baum, Willa, 96
Beard, Charles A., 89
Becker, Carl, 89, 92
Bethlehem Steel, 52
Blatti, Jo, 102
Bode, Carl, 104
Bohemia Manor, 53
Boswell, John, 95
Bowie State University, 57
Breslaw, Elaine, 104
Brugger, Robert J., 99, 104
Bryan, Charles Faulkner, Jr., 97
Butterfield, Herbert, 98

Callcott, George H., 100, 104
Calvert, Charles, third Lord Baltimore, 53
Calvert, George, first Lord Baltimore, 34
Calvert, Leonard, 34
Calvert family, 4, 5, 7; coat-of-arms of, 4; colors of, 4, 5, 7, 9

Cannery workers. *See* Working-class communities
Carr, Lois Green, 52, 62, 69, 76, 99, 104
Carroll, Charles, Barrister, 13
Carroll, Dr. Charles, 13
Carroll, Charles, of Annapolis, 13
Carroll, Charles, of Carrollton, 13-14, 18, 23-26, 29
Carroll, Charles, of Homewood, 14, 19
Carroll, Charles, the Settler, 14-18, 58-59
Carroll family (Catholic branch), 13-14, 18, 20, 22, 24, 25; papers of, 14, 17, 22, 25
Carroll family (Protestant branch), 13
Carroll House, 13
Carroll Mansion, 13, 23-29
Caton, Richard, 23, 29
Caton family, 26
Cecil County, 52-53
Census records, 69-73, 77, 83, 84, 85, 101; schedules, 71-72
Ceramics, 19, 26, 33, 40
*Chronicle of Higher Education*, 101, 102
Churches, African-American. *See* African Americans, institutions of
Civil War, 5, 7, 8, 11, 92
Claiborne, William, 40
Clothing, 11, 58
Collections, 102-3
Collingwood, R. C., 89, 92, 98
Collins, Naomi, 105
Colonial Williamsburg, 75
Confederate Museum, Richmond, Va., 8
Confederates, 4, 5, 7, 8, 9
Coppin State, 57
Cordea's Hope (archaeological site), 34
Country's House (archaeological site), 34

*Critic, The,* 46
Court records, 15
Croce, Benedetto, 89
Cross bottony, 4, 5, 7, 8, 9, 11
Crossland family, 4, 5, 7; colors of, 4, 7, 8, 9, 11

Declaration of Independence, 24, 27
Department of Agriculture, 35
Diaries, 25, 83
*Dinner Party, The,* 26
Directories, city, 83, 84, 85
Dix, Gen. John, 9
"Dix's Manifesto," 10
Doughoregan Manor, 13, 18
Doughoregan Valley, 18
Drawings, 7

1840 House, 77-81
Elk River, 53
Elkton, 52
Environmental Protection Agency, 35

Farm Security Administration, 40
Farmers, yeoman, 58-60
Fells Point, 42, 72, 82
Fifth Maryland Regiment, 7
Fischer, David Hackett, 98
Flag, Maryland, 4-5, 7, 9, 11
Flags, 7, 8
Fry, Joshua, 53

Ghosting, 20, 22
Gilman School, 20
Ginzburg, Carlo, 95
Glass, 33; bottle seal, 33
Godiah Spray tobacco plantation, 74
Goldsborough, Jennifer, 81, 82, 83
Goldstein, Louis, 96
Green, Constance, 57
Griffith, Dennis, 53
Gude, Gilbert, 40, 49, 50, 105

108    Index

Heaney, Paddy, 18
Hegel, Georg, 89
*Henrietta Bach,* 39
Herbert, James R., 9
Herrman, Augustine, 53
Higham, John, 98
Hine, Lewis, 42, 44
Historic house museums, 18-29; interpretation of, 23-29; restoration of, 19-22
Historic St. Mary's City, 31, 74-77
Historiography, 98
History: local, 90, 96-98; social, 90
Hoffman, Ronald, 14, 17, 58, 105
Homewood House, 13, 18-22, 31
*House Servant's Directory, The,* 26
Hrabowski, Freeman, 105
Hubard, William, 25
Hundley, Paul, 39, 105
Hutchinson, John, 77

Interpretation, in historic house museums, 23-29; through living history, 74-81
Inventories. *See* Probate records

Jefferson, Peter, 53
Johns Hopkins University, 18
Johnson, Gen. Bradley, 8
Johnson, Joshua, 81-85
Jones, Dale, 78

Kant, Immanuel, 89
Kempton, 40-41, 49-50
Kent Island, 40
Kessler, Barry, 23, 105
Kettlewell, Charles, 8
Key, Francis Scott, 80
Knights of Labor, 47
Kummerow, Burton K., 74, 78, 105
Kyvig, David, 98

Lade, Peter, 35, 40, 105
Land records, 15, 60

Landscapes, 17
Leone, Mark, 105
Letters, 14, 17, 20, 25, 26, 83
Library of Congress, 40, 103
Living history, 74-81; flexibility of, 78-80
Lowenthal, David, 99

McGovern, Charles, 105
Malloy, Margaret, 80
Maps, 32, 34, 49, 52-53
Marling, Karal Ann, 99
Martenet, Simon, 53; map of, 71
Marty, Myron, 98
Maryland Department of Agriculture, 52
Maryland Historical Society, 11, 81, 103
Maryland Historical Trust, 39, 40
*Maryland Humanities,* 96
Maryland Humanities Council, 1, 90, 96
*Maryland Line Confederate Soldier's Home,* 8
Maryland State Archives, 102-3
Mayer, Frank B., 7
Memorabilia, Civil War, 8
Migrant workers. *See* Working-class communities
Miller, Henry, 31, 58, 76, 106
Mining communities. *See* Kempton
Morgan State University, 57
Mt. Clare, 13
Museums: industrial, 85-88, interpretation in, 86-88. *See also* Historic house museums

National Archives, 103
National Association for the Advancement of Colored People (NAACP), 57
National Child Labor Committee, 44
National Museum of American History, 102, 103

National Oceanic and Atmospheric Administration, 35
National Trust for Historic Preservation, 102
Newsome, Steven C., 44, 53, 53, 57, 58, 106
Newspapers, 44-49, 84; African-American, 45-46; as sources for working-class history, 46-49

O'Carroll family, 17, 18
Old Town, 82
Oral history, 40, 44, 49-52, 95-96
Organization of American Historians, 101, 102
*Our Town*, 94-95

Paintings, 26, 81
Papenfuse, Edward C., 106
Papers, family, 13, 14, 17
Photographs, 7, 20, 40, 41-44, 53, 96
Pickersgill, Mary, 80
Point papers, 22
Port Deposit, 52
Portraits, 25, 82-84
Potomac River, 40
Probate records, 58, 62, 84; accounts, 62; inventories, 15, 20, 29, 58-60, 62-66, 77; wills, 60-62
Proceedings, Maryland legislature, 17

Roberts, Robert, 26
Russo, Jean B., 106

Salisbury State University, 35, 38
Sargent, Henry, 26
Satellite data, 38
Schulz, Constance B., 96
Shopes, Linda, 41, 46, 49, 50, 72, 96, 106
Slaves, 58; of Charles Carroll, 29

Slieve Bloom mountains, 17
Smith's Tavern (archaeological site), 34
Smithsonian Institution, 103
Soil Conservation Service, 52
St. Mary's City, 32-34, 35, 74, 75
St. Mary's County, 75
Stiverson, Gregory A., 106
*Sun*, 46
Susquehanna River, 52

Tax records. *See* Assessments
Technology, modern, 35-38, 39-40; computers, 35, 38, 39, 65-66, 101
Teleiback, Clara, 11
Thompson, Paul, 96
Tindeco Wharf, 51
Tobacco pipes, 33
Travel accounts, 25
Tripp, Susan, 18, 19, 31, 106

University of Maryland-Eastern Shore, 57
Urban League, 57

Voting lists, 101

Walsh, Lorena S., 59, 60, 66, 106
Warren, Marion E., 96
Warren, Mame, 96
Washington, George, 92, 99
Weidman, Gregory, 81, 82, 83, 84, 85
Western Maryland. *See* Kempton
Wetherington, Mark V., 97
Wills. *See* Probate records
Working-class communities, 41-44, 46-49, 50-52, 72-73, 77
Wyman family, 20

Young, Alfred, 102

Zelinsky, Wilbur, 99
Zembala, Dennis, 86, 87